HBJ Reading Program

Margaret Early

Bernice E. Cullinan
Roger C. Farr
W. Dorsey Hammond
Nancy Santeusanio
Dorothy S. Strickland

LEVEL 8

Sunbeams

HBJ **HARCOURT BRACE JOVANOVICH, PUBLISHERS**
Orlando   San Diego   Chicago   Dallas

Acknowledgments

For permission to reprint copyrighted material, grateful acknowledgment is made to the following sources:

Atheneum Publishers, Inc. and Artemis Verlag: Adapted from *The Miser Who Wanted the Sun* by Jürg Obrist. Copyright © 1983 by Artemis Verlag/Flash, Zürich and Munich. English translation copyright © 1983 by Methuen Children's Books Ltd. A Margaret K. McElderry book.

Eleanor Clymer: From *The Spider, the Cave and the Pottery Bowl* (Titled: "The Cave") by Eleanor Clymer. Published by Atheneum Publishers, Inc., 1971.

Coward, McCann & Geoghegan: Adapted from *The Desert: What Lives There* by Andrew Bronin. Text copyright © 1972 by Andrew Bronin.

Dodd, Mead & Company, Inc.: From *The Buried Treasure*, retold by Djemma Bider. Copyright © 1982 by Djemma Bider.

Dover Publications, Inc.: "The Corn-Grinding Song," a poem of the Zuñi Indians from *The Indians' Book*, edited by Natalie Curtis. Published by Dover Publications, Inc., New York, 1968.

E. P. Dutton, a division of New American Library: Adapted from "The Case of the Cave Drawings" in *Encyclopedia Brown Keeps the Peace* by Donald J. Sobol, illustrated by Leonard Shortall. Copyright © 1969 by Donald J. Sobol.

Lydia Freeman: From *Hattie the Backstage Bat*, story and pictures by Don Freeman. Copyright © 1970 by Don Freeman. Published by Viking Penguin Inc.

Harcourt Brace Jovanovich, Inc.: From *HBJ Science*, Level Green, Grade 3 by Elizabeth K. Cooper et al. Published by Harcourt Brace Jovanovich, Inc. Cover illustrations from *Big Anthony and the Magic Ring; The Prince of the Dolomites; Strega Nona's Magic Lessons;* and *Sing, Pierriot, Sing* by Tomie dePaola. Copyright © 1979, 1980, 1982, 1983 by Tomie dePaola. Pronunciation Key from p. 33 and the short key from p. 35 in *HBJ School Dictionary*. Copyright © 1985 by Harcourt Brace Jovanovich, Inc.

Harcourt Brace Jovanovich, Inc. and Methuen Children's Books Ltd.: Abridged and adapted from *Hilda the Hen Who Wouldn't Give Up* by Jill Tomlinson. Text copyright © 1967, 1977 by the Estate of Jill Tomlinson.

Harper & Row, Publishers, Inc.: Abridged and adapted from Chapter 3 of *Bicycle Rider* by Mary Sciosia. Copyright © 1983 by Mary Sciosia.

Houghton Mifflin Company: Adapted from *Encore for Eleanor*, written and illustrated by Bill Peet. Copyright © 1981 by William B. Peet. Adapted from *Merle the High Flying Squirrel*, written and illustrated by Bill Peet. Copyright © 1974 by William B. Peet.

The Instructor Publications, Inc., New York, NY 10017: "The Wheel" by Josephine Van Dolzen Pease, "The Painting Lesson" by Frances Greenwood, and "The Spider Web" by Truda McCoy from *Poetry Place Anthology.* Copyright © 1983 by The Instructor Publications, Inc.

Little, Brown and Company: Adapted from "Why Spider Lives In Ceilings" in *The Adventures of Spider*, retold by Joyce Cooper Arkhurst. Copyright © 1964 by Joyce Cooper Arkhurst. *Little Brown and Company in association with The Atlantic Monthly Press:* Adapted from *All Except Sammy* by Gladys Yessayan Cretan. Text copyright © 1966 by Gladys Yessayan Cretan.

Lothrop, Lee & Shepard Books, a division of William Morrow & Company, Inc.: Abridged and adapted from *The Great Town and Country Bicycle Balloon Chase* (Titled: "The Bicycle Balloon Chase") by Barbara Douglass. Copyright © 1984 by Barbara Douglass. Illustrations from pp. 2–3, 8, 21 and 25 by Carol Newsom. Copyright © 1984 by Carol Newsom. Entire text and illustrations from pp. 5, 10, 16, 24–25, and 32 in *Sam Johnson and the Blue Ribbon Quilt*, written and illustrated by Lisa Campbell Ernst. Copyright © 1983 by Lisa Campbell Ernst.

Macmillan Publishing Company: "Learning About Bar Graphs" from pp. 58–59 in *Communities, People and Places* by John Jarolimek, Senior Author, and Ruth Pelz. Copyright © 1985 by Macmillan Publishing Company, a division of Macmillan, Inc.

Margaret Mahy: From *The Dragon of an Ordinary Family* by Margaret Mahy. Text © 1969 by Franklin Watts, Inc. Published in the United States by Franklin Watts, Inc. and in Great Britain by William Heinemann Ltd.

McGraw-Hill Book Company: From pp. 115–117 and 138 in *Gateways to Science*, Book 3 by Neal J. Holmes et al. Copyright © 1983 by McGraw-Hill, Inc. Published by McGraw-Hill Book Company.

McIntosh & Otis, Inc.: From *Pornada* by Mary Francis Shura. Text copyright © 1968 by Mary Francis Shura.

Eve Merriam: "Shh" from *A Word or Two With You* by Eve Merriam. Copyright © 1981 by Eve Merriam. All rights reserved. Published by Atheneum Publishers, Inc.

G. P. Putnam's Sons: Adapted from *Now One Foot, Now the Other*, story and pictures by Tomie dePaola. Copyright © 1981 by Tomie dePaola. Cover illustration from *The Legend of the Bluebonnet*, retold and illustrated by Tomie dePaola. Cover illustration from *The Knight and the Dragon*, written and illustrated by Tomie dePaola. Copyright © 1980 by Tomie dePaola.

Random House, Inc.: "Alphabet Stew" by Jack Prelutsky from *The Random House Book of Poetry for Children*, selected and introduced by Jack Prelutsky. Copyright © 1983 by Random House, Inc.

Scott, Foresman and Company: From *City, Town, and Country* by Dr. Joan Schreiber et al. Copyright © 1983 by Scott, Foresman and Company.

Silver Burdett Company: From *The World and Its People: Communities and Resources* by Richard H. Loftin. © 1984 by Silver Burdett Company.

The Literary Trustees of Walter de la Mare and The Society of Authors, as their representative: "Seeds" by Walter de la Mare.

Yoshiko Uchida: From pp. 15–38 in *Sumi's Special Happening* by Yoshiko Uchida. Published by Charles Scribner's Sons, 1966.

Albert Whitman & Company: From *Words in Our Hands* by Ada B. Litchfield. Text © 1980 by Ada B. Litchfield. Published by Albert Whitman & Company.

(continued on page 328)

Contents

Unit 2 # Landscapes   **74**

Unit 3

Applause

146

Unit 4 # Windows

Sunbeams

Unit 1

Voyages

Have you ever thought about the different ways you can travel from one place to another? Of course you know that you can travel by land, by sea, or by air. Did you know that you can also travel in other ways?

Come along and travel with the characters in "Voyages." See where their voyages take them and what happens to them along the way. Join them as they travel far away or just around the corner.

As you read the stories in this unit, think about the voyage each character takes and how that voyage changes each character's life. When you turn the page, your voyage will begin!

What happens to Merle as he travels out West? What does he find when he gets there?

Merle the High-Flying Squirrel

story and pictures by Bill Peet

Merle was a shy little squirrel who lived in a big city park up in an oak tree. He hardly ever came down out of the tree. The noisy traffic and the tall gray buildings scared him. Even the people who came to the park frightened him.

"I'm tired of being scared," Merle said one morning. "It's no fun at all. From now on, I'm going to try and be brave enough to take a trip somewhere. I might go all the way across the park and back."

That same morning, Merle heard some people talking about all the places they had been and all the things they had seen.

"I've seen a lot of things," said one man. "However, nothing ever got me like the big trees out in the West. Why, some of them shoot up as tall as the tallest building. When you are standing there, you feel mighty small, not just small like here in the city. It's a good feeling. There's a great quietness about them. You've got to see them to understand what I mean."

After the people had gone, Merle sat up in the oak trying to picture a tree as tall as a building. "I just can't believe it," he said. "Not until I see one. So I must take a trip out West, but I don't dare run along the roads. The only safe way for a squirrel to travel is on the telephone wires."

So, with a sad "good-bye" to his oak tree, Merle took a flying leap over to the nearest telephone wire.

Then after making sure which way was west, he started off. High-wire walking was something new for Merle. He was not too steady at first. The noise of the traffic down below gave him the shakes.

"Remember," he said, "no more being scared. I've got to be brave! Brave!" Just like that, Merle got over the shakes. Soon he was running along the wires at a fast, steady clip.

"At this rate," he said, "the trip out West will be easy. I'll be there in a flash!"

Before he knew it, however, most of the day was gone. It was late afternoon and he was still in the city. Finally, Merle hopped to the top of a telephone pole to catch his breath and give his feet a rest. Suddenly he realized the trip was going to be too hard.

Merle sighed, "It is way too much of a trip for a squirrel. It would take forever."

So Merle gave up his dream of seeing the big trees and headed back for the park. By now, the sun was setting. It would be dark long before he reached the oak tree. So Merle began looking around for a safe place to spend the night.

Pretty soon he saw a big sign on the roof of a tall building. In one leap, he was on the roof. Then, picking out a huge letter S, Merle curled up in the bottom of the letter and fell sound asleep.

The next morning, Merle woke up to the sound of voices coming from somewhere below. He sat up with a shiver of fright.

"We could grab it by the tail," someone said, "if we could reach it."

In a flash, Merle was on top of the letter *S*. Looking down at the street, he spotted two boys, but they were not looking up at him. They were staring up at a kite tangled in the telephone wires.

"We had better get someone to help us," said one boy. "Let's go!"

As the boys raced away to get help, Merle had a bright idea. "I'll surprise them," he said. "I'll untangle the tail and have the kite down before they get back."

Then Merle hurried out onto the wires and set to work. He was so busy tugging at the tangle, he didn't notice the storm clouds rolling over the city. A fierce wind came up so quickly that Merle was caught by surprise.

Swoosh! The kite was swept off the wires with Merle clinging tightly to the tail. Suddenly he was sailing high over the buildings up into the black clouds. Now he was *really* scared.

Merle was afraid the kite might be ripped to pieces, and then down he would tumble into a street full of traffic. The boys had made a good, strong kite, however, and it sailed lightly along in the middle of the fierce storm.

For a second, there was a break in the clouds. Merle caught sight of the earth far below with a tiny speck of a house here and there. "I must be a mile high," thought Merle. "I'm on a flying trip, and it might be a long one if I can just hang on." He tightened his hold on the fast-moving tail.

At last, the fierce storm blew itself out. The wind died down to a whisper, and the kite dropped out of the clouds. The tail stopped moving and Merle found himself drifting down. All he could see below him were rocks and dry brush. There was no sign of a tree anywhere.

"No!" cried Merle, "not here! I couldn't stand to live here, not even for a day!"

Just as the kite was about to touch the ground, along came a whirlwind, swirling up clouds of dust. It caught the kite, and Merle was taken for another ride.

Then a powerful crosswind sent the kite sailing over high mountain peaks. "We've gone far enough," begged Merle, pulling at the kite tail. "Come down, you silly old kite!"

However, the kite kept sailing for hours, carried along by a lively breeze high over more mountain peaks and more forests.

Just before sunset, the kite began drifting down through rosy pink clouds. Merle noticed the kite was heading straight for the sea! He realized he had made the trip too far out West. "I'm done for," Merle groaned.

All at once, the kite stopped with a jerk. The tail had caught onto the tip of a runt of a pine tree. Merle hopped onto a branch for a look around.

Thick fog covered the ground. Here and there Merle saw a runt of a pine tree. "What a strange place," said Merle. "At least I'm lucky to have landed in a tree and not in the sea. Even if it is just a runt of a tree, it's a place to sleep."

When Merle woke up the next morning, he was so surprised he nearly tumbled off the branch. What a tumble it would have been! The fog had drifted away and Merle discovered he was high in the air, up in the very tip top of a huge redwood! On every side were more huge trees! He saw a whole forest of them!

"I can't believe it," cried Merle, "I'm here! I'm way out West in the big trees! They *are* as tall as buildings and a whole lot more beautiful. There is a great quietness about them. I feel mighty small out here, but not as small as I did in the city. It is a good feeling!"

1. What did Merle find when he got out West?

2. What three things did Merle see through the clouds as he traveled West?

3. After the fog lifted, what did Merle discover?

4. Find a clue in the story that made you realize that Merle thought the boys wanted to grab his tail.

5. Do you think that Merle was a lucky squirrel? Why?

Authors give clues in their stories that help the reader draw conclusions. Read the following conclusions. Then find details in the story that support each conclusion.

1. If Merle had not tried to untangle the kite, he would not have taken a trip on it.

2. Merle felt good about being out West.

Prewrite

Think about Merle's adventure. What happened as he traveled West? What things did he see? What frightened him?

Compose

Choose one of the activities below.

1. Write a paragraph describing three of the times when Merle was afraid during his trip. Tell what he was afraid of and how each of these problems was solved.

2. Pretend that you are Merle. Write a paragraph describing your trip. Tell what you saw and how you felt. Would you take the same trip again? Why?

Revise

Read your paragraph. Did you write a good description? Did you answer each of the questions? If not, revise your work to make your description complete.

Do you know that there are many different kinds of kites? Read to find out what some of them are and how they have been used.

Kites in Flight

by Cheryl Francis

Have you ever gone to a field to fly a kite on a bright, sunny day? Have you ever sat at the beach and watched a kite in flight? Have grown-ups told you stories about times when they flew kites?

Did you know that people began flying kites over two thousand years ago? The Chinese were the first people to invent and use kites. The kites they made were very beautiful. Some were shaped like fish, while others were made to look like dragons.

Sometimes the Chinese people flew kites just for fun. At other times they used kites to help them with their work. They tied a fishing line to the end of a kite. When a fish bit the bait, the kite moved. Then the kite and the fish were pulled in. Chinese farmers put kites in their fields to scare away birds that tried to eat their crops.

Most kites have three main parts: a frame, a cover, and a flying line. The frame may be made of wood or plastic sticks. The cover is often made of paper, plastic, silk, or nylon. These materials are used because they are so light. Thin nylon string, which can be wrapped around a stick, is used for the flying line.

A tail is used to stop a kite from spinning on a windy day. The tails may be made of cloth, paper, or feathers. The larger a kite is, the bigger its tail needs to be.

There are hundreds of different kinds of kites, but most kites fit into one of five main groups. The first kind of kite is the *flat kite*. It is made of two crossed sticks, which are covered with material. It has a tail. A flat kite, like all kites, must be made so that the right and left sides are exactly the same. If these sides are not exactly the same, the kite will not fly.

The *bow kite* is the name of the second kind of kite. It is a short, wide kite that is shaped like a bow. Most bow kites do not have tails.

The third kind of kite is the *box kite*. Box kites are shaped like a box. They are often very large. Since box kites do not spin, they do not need tails.

The fourth kind of kite, a *flexi-kite,* looks like a paper airplane. Since a flexi-kite does not have a frame, it bends and moves with the wind. Most flexi-kites do not have tails.

The last kind of kite, a *novelty kite,* may be made in many different shapes, colors, or sizes. Chinese-dragon kites, snake kites, and butterfly kites belong to this group. Bits of colored glass are sometimes tied to the kite's tail to make sounds as the kite flies.

Many famous people have flown kites. In 1752, Benjamin Franklin discovered electricity by flying a kite. The Wright brothers learned a lot about flying by watching box kites. This helped them to build their first airplane. Alexander Graham Bell, the inventor of the telephone, also made and flew kites. In 1907, he built a box kite that lifted a man 168 feet into the air! The man stayed in the air for seven minutes.

Today almost all kites are flown for fun. The next time you fly a kite, remember that you are doing something that people have been doing for thousands of years.

1. What kinds of kites are described in the selection?

2. How did the Chinese use kites?

3. What famous people flew kites?

4. Do you think you would like to fly a kite? Why?

5. Where in the story does it tell you that many different materials can be used to make kites?

Most kites have three main parts: a frame, a cover, and a flying line. Some kites also have a tail. Classify the kinds of kites in this selection into two groups: "Kites With Tails" and "Kites Without Tails." Use your book to help you.

Prewrite

Think about the kinds of kites that were described in the selection. Which kind do you like best? Why? What might you do if you owned that kind of kite?

Compose

Choose one of the activities below.

1. Write a paragraph describing a kite you would like to have. What would it look like? What would it be made of? Would it be used for fun or for work?

2. Pretend that you have flown a kite. Write a paragraph answering these questions. What kind of kite did you fly? Where did you go to fly it? What did you see in the sky as you flew the kite?

Revise

Check your paragraph to make sure you have answered each question in the activity you have chosen. Correct your work if necessary.

Adventure

Here's an adventure! what awaits
Beyond these closed, mysterious gates?
Whom shall I meet, where shall I go?
Beyond the lovely land I know?
Above the sky, across the sea?
What shall I learn and feel and be?
Open, strange doors, to good or ill!
I hold my breath a moment still
Before the magic of your look.
What shall you do to me, O Book?

—*Anonymous*

23

Newspapers

Look at the front page of the newspaper. Find the name of the paper and the date. Now find the name of the city and state in which the newspaper was printed. Notice that the first page also has the title of the most important story of the day. This title, called the **major headline,** is printed in larger letters. Notice that the headline is short and catchy. There are no unnecessary words in the headline. Writers try to make the headline interesting to get the reader's attention.

THE DAILY NEWS

CENTERVILLE, MAINE   September 14, 1984

Kittinger Lands Safely in Italy
—by Jack Williams

SAVONA, ITALY—Today Joe Kittinger did what he set out to do. He landed his big Balloon of Peace safely at six o'clock this morning, Orlando time, in the mountains of Savona, Italy. Kittinger became the first person to cross the Atlantic alone in a balloon.

The landing was not quite as Kittinger had planned. His foot was hurt when he was thrown ten feet from the balloon as it landed in the treetops. People living nearby took him to a doctor for help.

The ten-story Balloon of Peace took off last Friday evening at six o'clock from Caribou, Maine. Kittinger had a plan for a six day trip with him. As in many plans of this kind, the landing place was not given.

Shuttle Postponed
—by Karen Jones

Cape Canaveral, Florida — The launch of the space shuttle has been postponed due to a computer breakdown.

First Snowstorm Hits Maine
—by Anne Cooper

Caribou, Maine — The season's first snowstorm dumped seven inches of snow on surprised people in Caribou, Maine.

All other newspaper stories have headlines, too. These headlines are printed in letters smaller than those in the major headline. These headlines also use few words and are made interesting so people will read them.

Some news stories also have a **dateline,** which tells where the story was written. Long ago, the date also was given in the dateline because newspapers were printed weekly, not every day. The date was needed to let the people know when the story was written. Today, many newspapers are printed every day and the date does not need to be given for each story. The word *dateline* is still used, however.

Many news stories also have a **byline,** which tells who wrote the story. Usually bylines are not given for local news stories, very short news stories, or stories not needing much research.

Look at the headline, dateline, and byline for the true story about Joe Kittinger. The headline gets your attention and makes you want to read more. The dateline tells you that the story was written in Savona, Italy. Who wrote the news story? The byline tells you that a reporter named Jack Williams wrote the story.

Look for other news stories in newspapers. Use the headline, dateline, and byline to help you find newspaper stories you would like to read.

How does a bicycle race become an exciting voyage for both Gina and her grandfather?

The Bicycle Balloon Chase

by Barbara Douglass

"What does that mean?" Gina asked Grandpa, pointing to the poster. It was the third poster she'd seen that week. "What's a bicycle balloon chase?"

The man in the bike shop told them about it.
"A big hot-air balloon will take off from the
park this Saturday. Only the wind knows which
way it will go. We'll follow it on our bikes. After
the balloon lands, the first two bikers who get
close enough to touch it will win a free ride in it."

After breakfast each day, Gina and Grandpa
pedaled all over town. They rode uphill on
Main Street. They rode downhill on Maple
Street. Gina counted five more posters.
Grandpa counted shortcuts.

"Only the wind knows which way the balloon
will go," he said. "So we have to know the
shortest way to everywhere."

On Saturday Gina and Grandpa were up
before sunrise. After breakfast Gina packed
apples and peanuts while Grandpa pumped air
into their bicycle tires. At last Grandpa put on
his cap and said, "I do believe we're ready.
Let's go chase that balloon."

In the park Gina saw bicycles with great big
front wheels and little tiny back wheels. She
saw bicycles with two seats and four pedals.
She even saw something with only one wheel,
called a unicycle, but she didn't see a balloon.

Gina saw a woman with a parrot and a basket in the back of a pickup truck. "Where's the balloon?" asked Gina.

"Look in the back of that truck," Grandpa told her. "The woman is an aeronaut, the basket is a gondola, and the balloon is in that bag."

"I thought it was a *big* balloon," said Gina.

"It will be," said Grandpa. "Wait and see."

Gina waited. The aeronaut and her helpers unloaded the truck. They set the gondola on the grass and tipped it over. They opened the bag and pulled out a bundle of green, red, purple, and blue material, and they unrolled it and unrolled it.

The long, skinny bundle had a big mouth. Helpers held it open. The aeronaut turned on a fan. The bundle began to stretch.

Then the aeronaut turned on a burner. The balloon began to fill with air. Finally it stood up straight and tall. It was taller than ten buildings stacked one on top of another.

"Ready?" called the aeronaut.

"Ready!" answered the bikers.

The helpers let go of the ropes. The balloon floated up and away.

A man on a bicycle with a big front wheel said, "I think the wind will blow the balloon this way. Let's take Main Street."

A woman on a unicycle said, "I think the wind will blow the balloon this way. Let's take Maple Street."

A man and a woman on a bicycle built for two said, "This way," and "That way," both at once. They took a spill. Grandpa took a shortcut. Gina followed Grandpa.

When the balloon drifted this way, Grandpa took this shortcut. When the balloon drifted that way, Grandpa took that shortcut. Gina followed Grandpa through every shortcut in town.

The balloon drifted into the country. It led them past a dairy, a farm, and a ranch. There it drifted even lower. "Hurry, hurry," said Gina to Grandpa. "I think we might be first!"

Grandpa and Gina pedaled faster. When the balloon dipped down, they were ready to run to it. Then the aeronaut called, "Whoops! A bull! We'll have to look for a better place."

The burner hissed. The bull roared. The parrot squawked in fright. The aeronaut called, "Oh, no! Gypsy! You come back here!"

The parrot flew this way. The balloon blew that way. Gina followed the squawking parrot. Grandpa followed Gina. All the other bikers followed the balloon.

The parrot didn't take any shortcuts. It led them back past the ranch, all the way around the farm, and across the dairy before it landed on a giant sunflower. Gina climbed up and caught it.

Quickly, Gina and Grandpa turned their bikes around. They pedaled harder and faster than ever past the dairy and the farm and the ranch.

They were the last ones to reach the balloon. The winners were ready to take their ride. The burner hissed, and the balloon tugged at the ropes.

Suddenly the aeronaut called to her helpers, "Wait! Don't let go yet."

She pointed to Gina and Grandpa and said, "Please put your bicycles in the back of our chase truck and come over here."

They did. The aeronaut said, "There's room in the gondola for two more bikers. Anyone who is smart enough to catch my runaway parrot should have a chance to go up in my balloon. Welcome aboard!"

1. What is a bicycle balloon chase?

2. In what way was the bicycle balloon chase exciting for Gina and Grandpa?

3. Why were Gina and Grandpa the last ones to reach the balloon?

4. What did you think when Gina and Grandpa followed the parrot and not the balloon?

5. When did you realize that Gina and Grandpa were going to get a ride in the balloon?

Newspaper articles have headlines, datelines, and bylines. You can use headlines to help you find articles in the newspaper. Think of a headline for an article about "The Bicycle Balloon Chase" that would make someone want to read the article. Then make up a dateline and a byline to go with your headline.

Prewrite

Pretend that you are Gina. You and Grandpa have just chosen to follow the balloon instead of the aeronaut's parrot. What might happen?

Compose

Choose one of the activities below.

1. Write a paragraph telling how you think the story might have ended if Gina and Grandpa had chosen to follow the balloon instead of the parrot. Who might have won the race? What might have happened to the parrot?

2. You are floating in a hot-air balloon. Write an article with a headline, dateline, and byline describing three things you see. How do these things look?

Revise

Read your paragraph or article. Will it make sense to someone reading it? Make changes if they are needed.

Diagrams

Diagram of a Hot-air Balloon

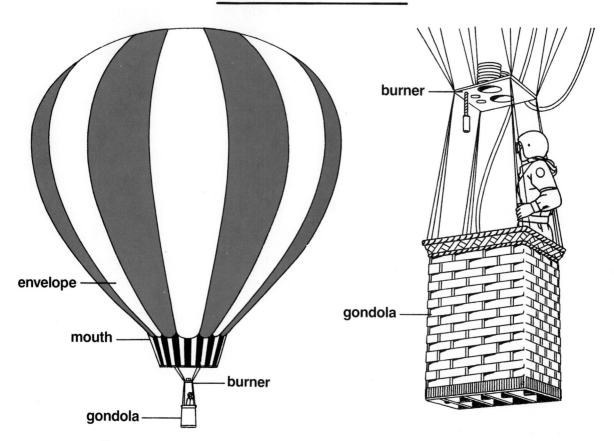

A **diagram** is a drawing used to explain how
something is put together or how it works. Some
diagrams have titles. The title of this diagram is
"Diagram of a Hot-air Balloon." All diagrams

have labels. Labels name the important parts of a diagram. They are connected by lines to the parts they name. What are the labels on this diagram? Did you answer *envelope, mouth, burner,* and *gondola?*

A diagram may have an **inset.** The inset shows details about one part of the diagram.

Look at the diagram on page 34. What is the largest part of the hot-air balloon? Yes, the envelope is the largest part. Notice that a line connects that part of the drawing with its label, *envelope.*

Now find the labels *burner* and *mouth* on the diagram. The burner heats the air by burning gas and making a flame. The mouth is the opening to the envelope. The air enters the balloon through the mouth. The envelope rises and floats high above the ground when the air in the envelope is heated.

Look at the inset. In which part of the hot-air balloon can people ride? Yes, people can ride in the gondola. How did you know? You can tell because a person is shown in the gondola on the diagram.

By using the diagram, you have learned about the main parts of a balloon. You have a better idea of how a hot-air balloon works.

Textbook Application: Diagrams in Science

Diagrams are often used in textbooks. They are used to make something easier to understand. Look at the diagram of a bicycle below. What is the title? Study the labels. What parts of the bicycle have been labeled? Now read the paragraphs on page 37. It will explain how the labeled parts of the bicycle work.

Diagram of a Bicycle

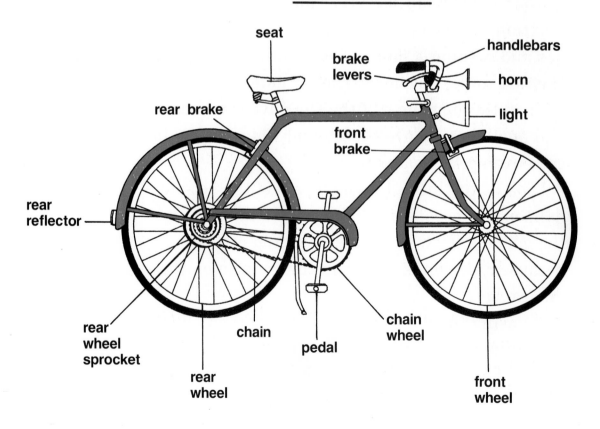

A bicycle has many parts. Some of them are the seat, the pedals, and the handlebars. Some safety parts are the brakes, a horn or bell, lights, and a reflector. The brakes help the bicycle stop. The reflector makes a bicycle easier to see at night.

A rider pushes the pedals up and down. The pedals are attached to a wheel called a chain wheel. The chain wheel has teeth on it. The pedals make the chain wheel go around. The chain wheel is attached by a chain to the rear-wheel sprocket. The chain moves when the chain wheel moves. The chain makes the rear-wheel sprocket turn. When the rear-wheel sprocket turns, the bicycle goes forward.

—*Gateways to Science*, McGraw-Hill

The diagram makes it easier for you to understand how a bicycle works. Having a picture of the important parts of a bicycle helps you understand the paragraph. Diagrams are useful for understanding how things work or how things are put together.

This selection is from a book about Marshall Taylor. Find out how a bicycle race changed his life.

Bicycle Rider

by Mary Scioscia

About a hundred years ago, a boy named Marshall Taylor got his first job in Mr. Hay's bicycle shop. There was a big bicycle race in Indianapolis each year. On the day of the big race, Mr. Hay asked Marshall to help him sell bicycles at the bicycle track.

As this true story begins, Marshall is watching excitedly while more than a hundred bicycle racers gather near the starting line.

"Attention everyone! All those in the first one-mile race line up at the starting line," a loud voice called.

"First one-mile race?" asked Marshall. "How many races will there be?"

"There will be several one-mile races before the main ten-mile race," said Mr. Hay. "Marshall, you just gave me an idea. You should ride in one of the one-mile races. I'll ask the judges if you can," said Mr. Hay.

When Mr. Hay came back, he said, "You can ride in the next one-mile race. Pick any of the bikes we brought."

At the starting line, Mr. Hay said, "Each time around the track is one lap. Five laps make a mile. Don't worry if you forget how many laps you've gone. When you hear the bell ring, you will know it is the bell lap. That means one lap left to go for the mile."

Marshall got on the bicycle and clipped his feet onto the pedals. A tall, thin boy in a red shirt got in line next to Marshall.

All the racers leaned over their handlebars. Their helpers held the bicycles steady. The starter raised his starting gun. "One! Two! Three!" the starter shouted. *Bang!*

Mr. Hay gave Marshall a strong push. He shot ahead. A tall boy got ahead of Marshall. Four more people got ahead. Marshall rode past one of them. He pushed his legs as hard as he could.

Around and around the racers went. Now there were seven people ahead of Marshall. *Ding, ding, ding,* the bell rang. Marshall knew that there was one more lap to go for the mile.

Marshall speeded up. One racer crossed the finish line . . . two more . . . another. Next was the boy in the red shirt. Right after him came the tall boy. Then Marshall crossed the line. Mr. Hay hurried over to help him stop.

"You came in number seven. That's great!" said Mr. Hay.

"It wasn't very good," said Marshall. "Six people beat me."

"You beat over forty people. You've never been in a race before. You're good enough to try the ten-mile race."

"Oh, no," said Marshall. "I could never win that."

"No," said Mr. Hay. "You couldn't win, but I think you could finish. Try it, Marshall. If you get tired, just stop. Many racers will drop out before the fifty laps are done."

During the last one-mile race, Mr. Hay spoke to the judges again. Marshall rested with several other riders in the middle of the track.

"Good news," said Mr. Hay, joining Marshall. "You can try the ten-mile race."

When the ten-mile race was called, Marshall wheeled his bicycle over to the starting line.

"Don't try to go too fast at first," said Mr. Hay. "Just keep up with the others, if you can."

Marshall's bike shook a little as he bent down to clip his feet onto the pedals. Mr. Hay steadied it.

Marshall could feel his heart thumping hard. His hands felt slippery on the handlebars. His legs felt shaky. "One!" shouted the starter. "Two! Three!" *Bang!*

Mr. Hay pushed the bicycle so hard, Marshall could smell the dust that flew up. Marshall pushed his legs around and around.

The riders rode in a close pack. Two bicycles bumped, and one fell. Marshall rode around the fallen bicycle and rider.

Marshall pulled ahead of the pack. The boy in the red shirt passed him. Three more riders passed him, then two more.

Marshall could hear the crowd cheering. It was hard to know who was ahead, because the riders kept going around and around the track. Around and around they went. Marshall's legs hurt. "I hope I can finish the first half of the race," he said to himself.

Marshall's mouth tasted dusty. "I want to drop out," he thought. "I can't make the halfway mark."

Someone shouted, "Hooray for Marshall Taylor!" It made Marshall feel stronger. "Maybe I can finish a few more laps," he thought.

His bicycle went faster and faster around the track. His wet shirt stuck to his back, and his back hurt from being bent over. His legs hurt, too.

The people in the crowd stamped their feet and cheered. Marshall heard Mr. Hay, standing at the edge of the track, shout, "Last lap coming up next!"

Marshall pushed as hard as he could. The wheels seemed to say, "Got to finish, got to finish."

Marshall speeded over the finish line. His bicycle was going so fast he couldn't stop. He went around another lap to slow down.

Marshall heard the crowd shout something that sounded like, "Marshall Taylor! Marshall Taylor!" Hats flew into the air.

Mr. Hay hurried over to Marshall. He hugged him. "You won, Marshall. You won the race!"

"Who, me?" asked Marshall.

The judges held up their hands to quiet the crowd. Then one shouted, "Marshall Taylor is the winner!"

Marshall Taylor became the fastest bicycle rider in the world. He was called Major Taylor because he stood so straight. He was the first black American to ride in bicycle races that had both black and white racers. From 1896 to 1910, Major Taylor raced in the United States and in many other countries. He held both American and world racing titles.

Bicycle racing was an important sport in the late 1800's and early 1900's. Huge crowds went to see any race Major Taylor rode in. All the newspapers covered the story.

Major Taylor was loved by his fans for his riding skills, his fairness, and his good sportsmanship.

1. How did a bicycle race change Marshall Taylor's life?

2. What were three ways in which Marshall was uncomfortable on the long bike ride?

3. Why was it a good idea for Marshall to ride in a one-mile race first?

4. What did the crowd do that helped Marshall?

5. When did you know that Marshall was going to win the ten-mile race?

A diagram shows how something works. On a sheet of paper, draw a diagram of a bicycle built for two. Label the seats, the handlebars, the pedals, and the reflector. Draw a line from each label to the correct part.

1. What helps the bicycle to be seen at night?

2. Which part helps to steer the bicycle?

Think and Write

Prewrite

Think about Marshall Taylor's ten-mile bicycle race. What helped him continue the race when he thought he could not go on? What made Marshall Taylor a special person? What part did Mr. Hay play in Marshall's life?

Compose

Choose one of the activities below.

1. Write a paragraph that lists at least two ways Mr. Hay helped Marshall Taylor get started as a bicycle racer.
2. Write a paragraph that tells at least three things that made Marshall Taylor a special person.

Revise

Read your paragraph. Will it make sense to someone reading it? Be sure you have written a main idea sentence and have listed at least three details that support the main idea of your paragraph.

The Wheel

by Josephine Van Dolzen Pease

How very strangely we should feel
If someone had not made a wheel!
No wagon would have crossed the plain,
No puffing engine, no speeding train.

No cart or carriage would there be,
Or roller skates for you and me,
No bicycle or automobile,
If someone had not made a wheel.

49

Fantasy

You have read many kinds of stories. Some of them were true to life and some were make-believe. One kind of make-believe story is called a **fantasy.**

A story may be a fantasy because of the characters in it. A story with talking animals, dragons, or giants is a fantasy. These characters do not exist in the real world. Authors have created them in their imaginations, and you can imagine them, too.

A story may also be a fantasy because of what happens in it. A story about a bicycle ride in the sky or a talking squirrel is a fantasy. These things could not happen in the real world, but we can pretend they happen in a story.

Read the following list of characters. Tell which ones are fantasy characters and why.

dragons   Gina and Grandpa   monsters
elves   Merle the squirrel   Marshall Taylor

Dragons, monsters, elves, and Merle the squirrel are fantasy characters because they can do things real people or animals cannot do. Gina, Grandpa, and Marshall Taylor are not fantasy characters. Gina and Grandpa do things that people can do in real life. Marshall Taylor was a real person.

Now read the sentences below. Tell which ones might be in a fantasy. Why?

1. A boy takes a bike ride over the treetops.
2. A girl finds a dog and takes it home.
3. A dog gets dressed and goes to work in his office.

Sentence 1 might be in a fantasy because a boy could not ride a bike over treetops in real life. Sentence 3 might be in a fantasy because a dog does not wear clothes or work in an office.

When you read a story, decide if it is a fantasy. Look for clues to tell when a story is make-believe. The main clues are the characters and the things that happen.

Hilda sets out to visit her aunt. What surprises does Hilda meet along the way?

Hilda, the Hen Who Wouldn't Give Up

by Jill Tomlinson

Hilda was a hen—a small, brown hen. She lived on Biddick's Farm in a village called Little Dollop.

Hilda was very excited. Her aunt had just hatched five baby chicks. Hilda couldn't wait to see them, but her aunt lived five miles away. How was Hilda going to get there? It was much too far to walk. She sat in her favorite spot under the hedge to think. Suddenly Hilda had an idea. Of course! She would have to get a ride.

Hilda squeezed through the thick hedge and hurried down the muddy lane from the farm. Anyone could see that she was a hen who was *going* somewhere.

She went down the farm lane and along the main road toward Much Wallop. She went right through the village of Little Dollop, and past the few houses on the other side. She found nothing she could ride except a wagon in somebody's front yard. That was not much good without somebody to pull it.

Then she saw the very thing! It was big and red, shining in the sun—and the driver was just getting into it. Hilda would ride on this.

The strange thing was that other people seemed to have the same idea! Several others jumped onto it at the same time as Hilda—people with shiny helmets. Hilda had no time to wonder why. She was too busy hanging on.

The fire engine—for that is what it was—had started off with great speed. Hilda was sure she would fall off. She closed her eyes tightly as the wind blew through her feathers. The big silver bell above her head began to clang and clang.

It was all very exciting! Hilda opened her eyes and looked around her. There was a ladder just above her. She could perch more safely on that. She climbed up to the ladder and hopped right to the top. She could see for miles from up there.

Hilda was excited. They would soon be at Much Wallop at this rate. Then, to her surprise, she saw that they were turning onto a side road. This was no good—she would have to get off.

"Stop!" she squawked. "Stop! I want to get off!" Of course, nobody heard her above the noise of the bell.

54

Then they did stop—suddenly. Hilda was nearly thrown off her perch at the top of the ladder. The ladder began to move. Before Hilda realized what was happening, she was going up and up into the air. The ladder was being sent up to the top windows of a very tall house. Now a fire fighter could climb up and save anybody who might be trapped on the top floor.

Poor Hilda was scared. The smoking windows were getting nearer and nearer, and she did not want to be a cooked chicken!

Then the ladder came to rest against the side of the house. Hilda was glad to find that she was not to be tipped right into the fire. She heard someone coming up the ladder behind her. She was just going to look around when—whoosh!—water hit the wall beside her. Hilda was soaked.

"Oh!" shouted a voice from behind. "Watch what you're doing with the hoses down there! It's not my night for a bath!"

Then the fire fighter saw Hilda—a little bundle of wet feathers perched at the top of the ladder.

"Hello!" he said. "What are you doing up here, young lady? You don't look like much of a fire fighter to me! I'll have you down quickly. Just hang on while I look around."

He was soon back again. "There's nobody there," he said. "Come on, down we go." He gently lifted Hilda off her perch, took off his helmet, and placed her in it. Hilda had a nice ride back to earth.

It was really very kind of him, especially as she was so wet. Hilda said "thank you" in the only way she knew—she laid a nice brown egg in his helmet! He felt it there when he put in his hand to lift her out.

"Well," he said, drawing it out. "Thank you!"

The fire was out, and the fire fighters were getting back on the engine to go home. "It's Hilda—from Biddick's Farm. We'd better take her home," the fire fighter said.

So Hilda had another ride on the fire engine—but quietly this time, in the kind fire fighter's helmet. He dried her as best he could, gently put her back into his helmet, and let the sun do the rest.

When they got to Little Dollop, Hilda's fire fighter set her down at the farm gate. She clucked softly to say good-bye and then squeezed under the gate and walked into the yard. It isn't every day that a hen comes home in a fire engine!

It was only after Hilda had told the others *all* about it that she realized that she still had not seen her aunt's new chicks at Much Wallop! She would try again tomorrow.

1. What surprises did Hilda meet as she traveled to visit her aunt's new chicks?

2. What problems did Hilda have after she got on the fire engine?

3. What problem did Hilda have that she did not solve?

4. Do you think the title fits the story? Why?

5. How did the author tell you that Hilda knew that the fire fighter had helped her?

Read the two sentences below. Sentence 1 is fantasy, and Sentence 2 tells something that could really happen.

1. Hilda yelled, "Stop! I want to get off!"

2. The fire engine went very fast.

Now find two more examples from the story that are fantasy.

Prewrite

The story you have just read is a fantasy because it is make-believe. What parts of the story are make-believe? What things could have really happened?

Compose

Choose one of the activities below.

1. Write a paragraph that tells about one thing that happened in the story that <u>could not</u> happen in real life. Add enough details to this to make the paragraph different from the story.

2. Write a paragraph that tells about one thing that happened in the story that <u>could</u> happen in real life. Add enough details to make your paragraph different from the story.

Revise

Check your work. Did you state the main idea of your paragraph? Did you write at least three details which support your main idea? If not, correct your work.

A dragon becomes the pet of an ordinary family. How does the dragon change their lives?

The Dragon of an Ordinary Family

by Margaret Mahy

There was a family called Belsaki—Mr. Belsaki, Mrs. Belsaki, and their little boy, Gaylord Belsaki. They were a quite ordinary family. Their house was a quite ordinary house on a quite ordinary street. They would have lived quite ordinary lives forever, if one morning Mrs. Belsaki hadn't called Mr. Belsaki a *fuddy-duddy.*

The day began with Mr. Belsaki rushing through his breakfast, a little late for work. As he was rushing out of the door, Mrs. Belsaki called after him, "On your way home, dear, stop in at the pet shop and buy Gaylord a pet."

"A pet!" cried Mr. Belsaki. "What does he want a pet for? We haven't the room, anyway."

"Of *course* he can have a pet," said Mrs. Belsaki. "We have room for an *elephant* if Gaylord wanted one."

"An *elephant*!" Mr. Belsaki turned a little pale.

"All right, all right," Mrs. Belsaki said, "he doesn't *want* an elephant. He just wants a puppy — or perhaps a little kitten. Don't be a *fuddy-duddy,* Mr. Belsaki!"

Mr. Belsaki stamped out, pulling his hat down over his ears, saying, "*Fuddy-duddy,* indeed!"

On his way home from work, Mr. Belsaki went into the pet shop and looked around. He saw white mice, cute puppies and kittens, all kinds of birds, and some sad-eyed goldfish. He also saw a parrot called Joe, with a sign over him saying "Not For Sale."

61

Then his eye caught a sign which said "Unusual Pet, Very Cheap." In smaller letters below, it said "Dragon, House-Trained, 50¢."

"That is a very good price," said Mr. Belsaki to the pet shop man. "I suppose it isn't a very good kind of dragon."

The pet shop man sighed. "No, it's a good kind— the *only* kind," he said. "Not very many people want dragons, you know."

Mr. Belsaki couldn't decide. The dragon winked its blue eyes at him. "I'll take it!" said Mr. Belsaki loudly.

That was how it happened that Mr. Belsaki came home with a tiny dragon in a tiny box.

"What on earth is in there?" Mrs. Belsaki asked.

"A dragon," said Mr. Belsaki.

"A dragon!" shouted Mrs. Belsaki.

"*A dragon!*" cried Gaylord.

"It's very unusual," Mr. Belsaki answered, "and it was cheap. You said I was a *fuddy-duddy,*" he added, "and I am no such thing!"

62

"You could have bought something pretty," Mrs. Belsaki said. "A kitten, perhaps, or a bird that talks. Where will we keep a dragon?"

"You said we have room enough here to keep an elephant," Mr. Belsaki told her. So they kept the dragon, and it grew and grew.

It was a wonderful pet for Gaylord. He kept it in the tiny box for a while, then in a bird cage, then in a dog house. He painted a washtub for its food, with the word "Dragon" on it in red.

The dragon grew and grew. Mrs. Belsaki became quite proud of it. "It certainly gives a different look to the place," she said at least once a day. "It makes us a bit unusual, too."

Her friends said, "What on earth did he get *that* for?" Mrs. Belsaki always answered, "Mr. Belsaki is a man with *ideas,* that's why!"

The dragon grew and grew. Finally it filled almost the whole yard. It got so it could breathe smoke and fire. It even got big enough for Gaylord to ride. Then it got as big as an elephant. None of Mrs. Belsaki's friends came to visit any more. They were quite afraid.

One day the Mayor came to look at the Belsakis' dragon. He studied and studied it. "It is much too big to keep in a built-up place," he said crossly. "Mr. Belsaki, you are just an ordinary family, and you should stick to ordinary pets. You must sell it to a zoo, or to a circus."

Mr. and Mrs. Belsaki looked very worried and sad. They loved their dragon, but it was getting too big. Besides, it cost so much to feed.

"We don't even have enough money to go on a vacation this year," Mr. Belsaki said sadly.

"I want to keep our dragon!" Gaylord cried.

"Well, you can't!" the Mayor answered. "You have exactly one week to get rid of it!" Then he went away.

Then the dragon turned around and faced them. For the first time, it spoke. "As a matter of fact, it *is* getting a little crowded here for me. How would you like to come for a vacation with *me* to the Isles of Magic?" the dragon asked. "*All* dragons know the way there."

Mrs. Belsaki thought a moment. "Well, it *could* be all right. I'll go and pack."

So the Mayor, Mrs. Belsaki's friends, and all their ordinary neighbors were surprised to see the Belsakis fly away on the dragon's back that very day with all their things tied to the dragon's tail.

Higher and higher the dragon flew—way up into the clouds. Then, after a long time, it dropped down, down, down. There, below them, lay a beautiful blue sea, with the Isles of Magic spread across it.

The Isles of Magic, the dragon told them as they flew along, are the homes of all the wonderful, strange, fairy-tale people. What would an ordinary family with an ordinary home do on the Isles of Magic?

They walked in the forests, the dark and old forests. They saw castles rising above the trees. They saw a princess sitting in the window of a castle combing her hair, waiting for a prince to come and save her.

They searched for gold on isles where parrots screamed in the tall trees. They saw giants that were as big as mountains.

At last the time came for them to go back home. The dragon stayed, for the Isles of Magic are the right place for dragons. As a good-bye present, the dragon gave Gaylord a tiny black kitten with an oversized purr. Then the Belsakis sailed off for home on a flying carpet.

"Now," said Mrs. Belsaki, her unpacking nearly done, "we can be ordinary people again. I was very fond of that dragon—but it will be nice to be with our neighbors again."

"Next year," Gaylord asked hopefully, "can we visit the Isles of Magic and see our dragon?"

"Who knows," said Mrs. Belsaki, a little sadly, "we may never see it again. I suppose we'll have to be just an ordinary family. Perhaps no other magic will ever happen to us again."

Just then the little black kitten woke and sat up tall in Gaylord's lap. "I wouldn't be too sure of that," it purred, and went back to sleep.

1. How did the Belsaki family become an unusual family?

2. What problems did the Belsaki family have after the dragon grew up?

3. How was the problem of getting rid of the dragon solved?

4. Do you think the Belsakis will ever be an ordinary family again? Why?

5. When did you think that it might be a good idea for the dragon to stay on the Isles of Magic?

Apply the Skills

Find three details in the story that support the following statement:

"The Dragon of an Ordinary Family" is a fantasy story.

Prewrite

In the story, the Belsakis had a very unusual pet. What is the most unusual pet you can think of? Would you like to have an unusual pet like the Belsakis' dragon? Why?

Compose

Pretend that you could have a dragon or another unusual pet. Draw a picture of this most unusual pet. Then, write a paragraph answering these questions. What is so unusual about your pet? What will it eat? Where will you keep your pet? What will you and your pet do? Why do you want this pet?

Revise

Check your work carefully to make sure you have answered each question in the activity. Correct your work if necessary.

Thinking About "Voyages"

In this unit, you learned that a voyage can take you far away from home or just around the corner. How was the bicycle ride that Gina and Grandpa took different from what they had planned? Marshall Taylor's race around a bicycle track did not turn out the way he thought it would. How did this voyage change Marshall's life?

Think about some of the other characters and the voyages that they took. On what voyages did the authors of these fantasies take you? Did the voyages end the way they were planned? Merle's voyage took him across the country on the tail of a kite. The Belsakis and their dragon flew away to the Isles of Magic. What adventure did Hilda have that she hadn't planned on having?

As you read other stories, look for voyages that the characters take. Are these voyages real or are they fantasies? Do the planned voyages change? What causes these changes?

1. *Voyage* is another word for trip. The characters in this unit had many adventures on the voyages they made. Which voyages are examples of fantasy? Why?

2. Which stories had voyages that were or could have been real? Why?

3. How was Hilda's voyage like Merle's voyage? How were their voyages different?

4. If Marshall Taylor had been in the same race as Gina and Grandpa, do you think he would have won? Why?

5. Which of the voyages in this unit would you like to take? Why?

Read on Your Own

Wheels by Byron Barton. Harper. This book tells about how the wheel was invented. It also tells why wheels are important and how we use them.

Hot-Air Henry by Mary Calhoun. Morrow. A cat stows away on a hot air balloon and ends up having the adventure of his life.

The Big Balloon Race by Eleanor Coerr. Harper. Ariel almost causes her famous mother to lose a balloon race. She ends up helping her to win it.

The Newspapers by Leonard Everett Fisher. Holiday. This book tells about the importance of newspapers in the 1800's and how newspapers helped to shape our country's ideas.

Bicycles: All About Them. Gribble McPhee. This book tells how bicycles work, and how to fix and take care of them.

His Finest Hour by David Neuhaus. Viking. Ralph hopes he will win a bike race and be asked to join the bicycle team. Look for the surprise ending in this book!

Eli by Bill Peet. Houghton. An old lion named Eli can't stand the vultures that live nearby. In the end, the creepy old birds teach him a lesson.

The Pinkish, Purplish, Bluish Egg by Bill Peet. Houghton. Read this book to find out what hatches from a strange egg.

The Glorious Flight Across the Channel with Louis Bleriot by Alice and Martin Provensen. Viking. This book tells the story of the man who crossed the English Channel by plane in the early 1900's in thirty-seven minutes.

Bicycle Rider by Mary Scioscia. Harper. The story you just read was taken from this book. Read it to find out more about Marshall Taylor and how he began bicycle racing.

Hilda, the Hen Who Wouldn't Give Up by Jill Tomlinson. Harcourt Brace Jovanovich. The story you just read was taken from one chapter in this book. Read it to find out more about Hilda's funny adventures.

Unit 2
Landscapes

Landscapes are all that you see around you. Tall mountains, deserts, and sparkling waterfalls are part of the landscape. Fields of tall grass and blue-green oceans are part of the landscape, too.

Some people paint landscapes, while others take pictures of them. Some people write poems about landscapes, while others write songs. Did you ever think that the same landscape might be seen differently by different people?

As you read the stories in this unit, think about how landscapes play important parts in the characters' lives. What do the characters learn from their landscapes?

Eleanor the circus elephant is unhappy after she is sent to live at the zoo. How does Eleanor solve her problem?

Encore for Eleanor

story and pictures by Bill Peet

Eleanor the elephant had been a great circus star for forty years. The huge elephant put on such a great act that she always left the crowd calling for more. "Encore! Encore!" everyone shouted. "Come on, Eleanor! Once more!"

76

Then one night, Eleanor suddenly lost her balance. Down she tumbled, to hit the floor in one huge *kerthunk!* As she lay there, everyone thought the old elephant had broken every bone. She wasn't hurt much, but the circus boss decided that Eleanor was no longer fit to stay in the show. So Eleanor was sent to live in the city zoo.

Eleanor was put into a pen with plenty of hay and water. Her elephant house was a neat red barn shaded by a big tree. "I'm lucky to be here," said Eleanor, "yet I'll never be happy unless I can perform a few tricks to earn my keep."

When people stopped at Eleanor's pen to stare at her, Eleanor felt silly just standing there. Without her fancy circus robe, she felt like an overgrown wrinkled ugly big bloop of a thing.

"If I can't look my best," Eleanor grumbled, "then I don't want to be seen at all." So Eleanor stayed out of sight as best she could.

It was a lonely life for an elephant who loved cheering crowds, bright lights, and lots of excitement. Eleanor would have gone on being lonely if someone had not come along to change things.

One day a girl came to the zoo to sketch the animals. As she set up her easel, she woke Eleanor from her afternoon nap. Eleanor had often wondered how people drew pictures. So she went across her pen to the fence, where she peeked over the girl's shoulder.

The girl was drawing the rhinoceros who lived in the pen just across the way. With a few quick strokes of her charcoal she drew the sleepy half-open eye, the stumpy horn, and the low jaw. She even put the hair on the tips of the ears! The girl's mind was made up to make her drawing as realistic as she could. So every now and then she stopped to look at the rhinoceros and decide where to put all the folds in his wrinkled skin.

Just when she was ready to draw his back legs, the rhinoceros flopped on the ground. He began rolling over and over on his back.

"Oh, no!" cried the girl. "Why couldn't that rhinoceros stay put!" She was so disappointed that she threw her charcoal onto the sidewalk. She picked up her drawing and threw it into a trash can. Then she went off to watch the ducks.

Eleanor was disappointed, too. She was about to head back to her barn, when she discovered that the charcoal was within easy reach. The sketch pad and easel were also nearby.

Suddenly Eleanor wanted very much to draw a picture. She looked to make sure that the girl was still watching the ducks. Then Eleanor took the charcoal in her trunk. Eleanor quickly drew the very first thing that came to mind—the face of Zonko the clown she remembered from the circus. To start off, she made two crisscrosses for eyes, two silly eyebrows and a long pointed nose, then a crooked grin.

Eleanor's drawing was far better than she thought it would be. She smiled to herself as she drew Zonko's big ears. Then she put a tall hat on his head. Eleanor was nearly finished when suddenly she was caught by surprise.

"I can't believe it!" cried the girl, pulling the drawing off the sketch pad. Then, waving Eleanor's clown drawing in the air, the girl shouted at the top of her voice, "Come look! Come look, everyone! Come see what this elephant drew!"

In no time at all a group of school children and their teacher ran over. They were very excited. Then the zookeeper stepped in.

"I hate to spoil your fun," he said, "but I'm afraid an elephant can't draw a picture. Even though Eleanor was once a circus performer, she is still just an animal."

"Just an animal, am I?" Eleanor grumbled. "I'll show him a thing or two!"

Once again Eleanor took the charcoal in her trunk. As everyone watched in surprise, Eleanor quickly dashed off a picture of a lion. It was old Maynard from the circus—sad eyes, whiskers, and all. She finished the sketch in only seventeen seconds!

"Great!" cried the zookeeper. "If Eleanor can draw a clown and a lion, she can draw lots of things! What do you say we put on an elephant-drawing show?"

Everyone happily agreed. Of course Eleanor was thrilled at the chance to be a star performer once more.

In less than a week, a special stage was built for the show. An extra-large easel was set up to hold extra-large sketch pads. Now Eleanor could make extra-large drawings for hundreds of children to see. Best of all, Eleanor was given a fancy new robe. Now she could look her best while she performed her act.

At the end of each show, the children always called for more. "Encore, Eleanor! Encore!" they shouted. "One more, Eleanor! Please! Draw one more!" That was sweet music to the happy old elephant's big flappy ears.

1. What were three reasons Eleanor was unhappy?

2. How did Eleanor solve her problem?

3. Who helped Eleanor solve her problem?

4. Do you think the title is a good one? Why?

5. How did you know that Eleanor wouldn't be lonely anymore?

An *effect* is something that happens, and a *cause* is the reason that something happens. Each incomplete sentence below states an effect in the story "Encore for Eleanor." On another sheet of paper, complete each sentence by writing the cause.

1. Eleanor watched the girl drawing the picture because ▒▒▒▒.

2. Eleanor drew Maynard the lion because ▒▒▒▒.

82

Prewrite

Think about why Eleanor felt so lonely. What happened to make Eleanor feel good about herself? What zoo animals could have helped Eleanor not be so lonely? How?

Compose

Choose one of the activities below.

1. Imagine that you are Eleanor and you have just been moved to the zoo. Pretend that you can write. Write at least three sentences telling the zookeeper how you feel, and why you aren't happy.

2. Imagine that you have just taken a trip to the zoo. Write a paragraph describing three things you saw there.

Revise

Read your paragraph carefully. Your paragraph should help someone else understand how you felt or what you saw. Make any changes in your work that are needed.

This article tells about an artist who lived long ago. Who was he? What did he most like to paint?

Claude Monet
by Anne Maley

The Man in the Boat

It was a sunny morning on the river. The water slapped softly at a boat moving through the water. A man was rowing the boat, but he was not a fisherman on his way out to catch a fish. He was an artist on his way out to paint a landscape. The boat was his floating studio, or working place.

The man found a spot on the river and began to set up his easel. Then he watched and waited.

When the light looked just right, he began to paint. He covered his white canvas with the colors of trees, water, and sky. When people looked at his painting later, he wanted them to see what he had seen—an early summer morning on the river.

The man in the boat lived long ago in France. He was an artist who loved the outdoors. Most of all, he loved the water. His name was Claude Monet. He is known as one of the greatest landscape painters who ever lived.

The Young Artist

Claude Monet was born in France in 1840. He spent his early years in a town where a great river ran into the sea. Claude loved the sea.

As a child, Claude was always sketching. People liked Claude's sketches. By working hard, Claude could sketch eight pictures a day and sell them.

By the time he was fifteen, Claude was already a famous artist in his home town. He sold his sketches to a shop, which hung them in the window. The shop also showed the work of another artist, named Mr. Boudin.

One day the two artists met at the shop. Mr. Boudin said to Claude, "So, young man, it's you who does these little sketches. They have something in them, but why not try painting? I will be happy to give you lessons."

At first Claude had no answer. He didn't like Mr. Boudin's paintings. He wasn't sure that he wanted Mr. Boudin to teach him to paint. Finally, Claude agreed.

Mr. Boudin taught Claude how to paint sunlight and shadows. He taught Claude a great deal about painting. When the lessons ended, Claude knew that he wanted to be a painter for the rest of his life. At the age of seventeen, Claude went to the city of Paris to study more about art.

The Difficult Years

Art school was not what Claude had expected. The teachers at art school said that artists should paint in studios, not outdoors. They had many rules for what to paint and how to paint it. Claude could not follow these rules. He said, "I can paint only what I see."

Claude became very unhappy. He finally left Paris, but he held onto his ideas, and he kept on painting. Claude painted landscapes in parks, near rivers, and beside the sea.

Claude also painted large pictures, like "Women in the Garden." He painted this picture on a canvas that was eight feet tall. First he painted as much of the canvas as he could reach. Then he connected wires to the canvas. He dug a hole and lowered the canvas into the hole. After he had painted the top of the canvas, he used the wires to lift the canvas out of the hole. The painting was finished.

Years went by. Claude painted many pictures, but he sold very few. Still, Claude never gave up. He loved his work and hoped that one day others would love it, too.

The Water Garden

When Claude Monet was forty-two years old, he and other artists had a large show in Paris. Monet's paintings were among the best-selling works in the show. Monet felt proud and happy.

After that, Monet and his family moved to a house in the country. Monet planted two gardens that are still there today. One was a flower garden. The other was a water garden.

Monet made his water garden in the shape of a pear. Around the sides he grew many kinds of flowers and trees. Then he built a high wooden bridge across one end. Water lilies of many colors floated in the water. When it was done, Monet called his garden "a mirror of the sky."

Monet found great happiness in looking at his gardens and in painting them. His last great work was a group of eight paintings of the water garden called *Water Lilies*. He painted these as a gift to France, his country. Today these paintings still hang in a special place in Paris.

Each of the eight paintings shows a different part of the water garden. As you move from one painting to another, you seem to walk around the garden from beginning to end. Because of the way Monet painted these works, you see the garden from morning until night. Walking among these paintings is like spending a whole day in Claude Monet's garden.

Monet painted his *Water Lilies* until the day he died at the age of eighty-six. He was almost blind, but he kept on painting. He did not just want to paint, he needed to paint. As he put it, "I paint just as a bird sings."

Discuss the Selection

1. Who was Claude Monet?

2. Why is Claude Monet still remembered?

3. What was Claude Monet's last great work?

4. Why do you think the author used subheads in this selection?

5. When did you realize that Claude Monet had his own ideas about things?

Apply the Skills

Descriptive details help us "see" things in our minds. Read the following sentences from "Claude Monet." Decide which sentence describes something, and which sentence tells about something but does not describe it.

1. It was a sunny morning on the river.

2. One day the two artists met at the shop.

Prewrite

Think about the sights and sounds you might see and hear in a water garden or on a river. What sights might be the same in both places? What sights and sounds might be different?

Compose

Choose one of the activities below.

1. Draw a picture of a water garden. Then write a paragraph describing that garden. Remember to tell about the flowers and anything else in your drawing.

2. Pretend you are with Claude Monet in his rowboat on the river. Write a paragraph describing what you might see, hear, and feel while you are out on the river with Monet.

Revise

Read your paragraph. Make sure that your description includes details. If not, revise your work and add details.

The Painting Lesson

by Frances Greenwood

Red and blue make purple;
Yellow and blue make green.
Such a lot of colors
To paint a lovely scene.

Pink and blue make orchid;
Black and white make gray.
Now I'll dry my brushes
Until another day.

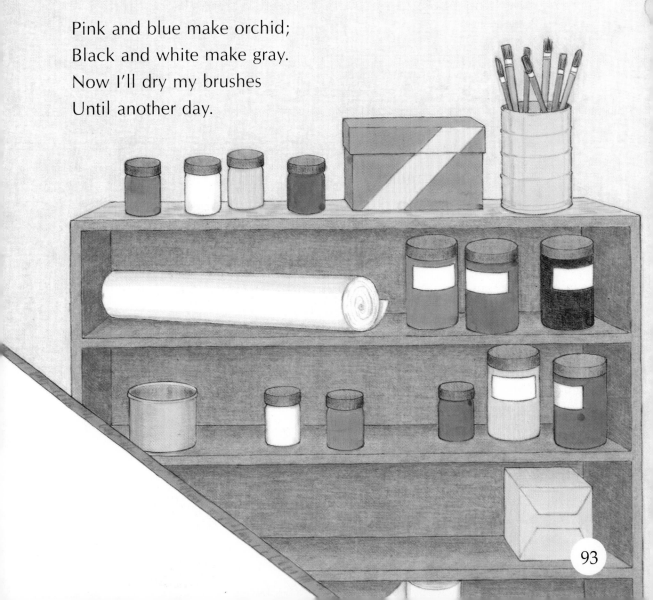

Outlines

Have you ever written a shopping list or a list of "things to do today"? Why did you write a list? Did you write it to help you organize information?

Read the following paragraph. Then look at the list that follows. How are the two alike?

Margie went shopping. She went to a department store and bought a skirt, shoes, and a lamp. Then she went to the grocery store. She bought bread, eggs, and milk. Margie's shopping list looked like this:

Shopping List

Department Store	Grocery Store
skirt	bread
shoes	eggs
lamp	milk

Margie's list tells the same things as the paragraph, but the list is easier to read. An organized list helps Margie remember what she

formation that you

nized list, or **outline.**

lication:

ience

a science textbook.

building

people have found many ways to use it. It is strong. Roads are made from it. So are some bridges, dams, and houses. Often, granite, marble, and limestone rock are used in buildings. Many tall office buildings in cities are made from rock.

There are many beautiful rock formations in our national parks. People come from all over the world to visit the Grand Canyon in Arizona and Yosemite National Park in California.

—*Gateways to Science*, McGraw-Hill

What are these two paragraphs about? Did you say *rock*? What does the first paragraph tell you? Yes, it tells about the uses of rock. What does the second paragraph tell you? Yes, it tells where to find beautiful rock formations. Here is a way to organize this information:

Rock
  I. Uses of rock
 II. Beautiful rock formations

This organization is called an **outline.** The title of the outline is "Rock." The main idea of the first paragraph, uses of rock, is one main topic of the outline. The main idea of the second paragraph, beautiful rock formations, is the other main topic of the outline. Notice that each main topic of the outline has a Roman numeral in front of it. Each Roman numeral is followed by a period. Notice that the main topics are groups of words. A main topic can be a single word, a group of words, or a sentence.

Now read the information on page 97 from another science book. Look for the main idea of each paragraph.

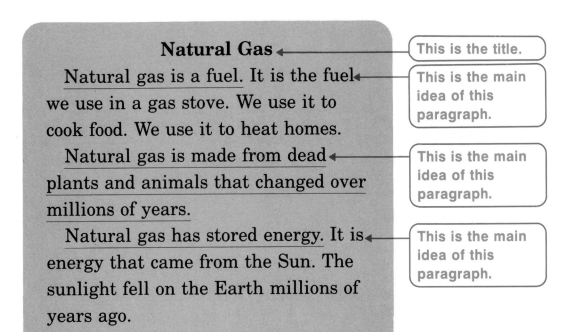

Natural Gas ← This is the title.

Natural gas is a fuel. It is the fuel ← This is the main idea of this paragraph.
we use in a gas stove. We use it to
cook food. We use it to heat homes.

Natural gas is made from dead ← This is the main idea of this paragraph.
plants and animals that changed over
millions of years.

Natural gas has stored energy. It is ← This is the main idea of this paragraph.
energy that came from the Sun. The
sunlight fell on the Earth millions of
years ago.

—*HBJ Science (Green)*, Harcourt Brace Jovanovich

Tell how you would complete the outline below using the information and sidenotes from above. Remember, the main idea of each paragraph will be the main topics of the outline. Main topics can be single words, groups of words, or complete sentences.

Natural Gas

  I. Natural gas is a fuel.
 II. ▬▬
III. ▬▬

Organizing information will help you remember what you read. An outline is one way to organize information.

What is the old Mexican legend? How does a pig help to prove it?

Pornada

by Mary Francis Shura

After the long, cold winter, spring was almost too beautiful to believe. As if by magic, the hills of Mexico were bright with color.

Each afternoon Francisco would race home from school. This gave him more time to play in the hills with his pet pig, Pornada. Sometimes Francisco's little sister, Josi, came along.

One day, as they were going home for supper, Francisco and Pornada stopped suddenly. They saw a tall man coming down the road.

"Guido!" Francisco cried, "Guido, my friend!"
Off he ran toward Guido with Pornada racing
behind him. Josi, who was riding on Pornada's
back, held on tightly to Pornada's ears. She cried,
"Stop! Stop!" at the top of her voice.

Guido looked up the trail at them. His face
changed quickly from sadness into a smile and
then into a shout of laughter. He walked quickly
toward them and lifted Josi from Pornada's back.
He patted her hair and hugged her, still laughing.

"Welcome back, Guido," Francisco said as he
jumped with joy. "How we have missed you!"
Pornada sat up straight on his back legs. He
seemed to be welcoming Guido home, too.

"Come for supper," Francisco begged. "Mama
and Papa would be so happy to see you."

Guido said no, but the children were able to get him down the hill. Mama and Papa, watching from the doorway, welcomed him inside.

"You have traveled a long time, Guido the Gem Finder," Francisco said.

"Perhaps you should call me just *Guido* now," his friend sighed. "In all those travels I did not find the gem I was searching for. So many miles I have traveled." He sighed again.

"You found no jade?" Mama asked.

Guido shook his head. "I was so sure that for once an old legend would come true!"

"There is a legend about this jade?" Papa asked.

Guido laughed. "Such a legend. I should have laughed at it long ago. They say that where jade lies sleeping under the earth, a mist rises at dawn. They say that it is the jade itself breathing through the stone. Only artists and dreamers would believe such a tale, but I believed it. In rain and sun I have searched every dawn, and still my hands are empty."

"Francisco goes out at dawn, too," said Mama, "but he goes out to paint."

"What great sights your eyes must have seen," Papa said thoughtfully.

"Indeed they did," Guido agreed. "I have visited the caves of the Indians and walked through beautiful cities."

"But never," Francisco asked, "never once did you see the stones breathe at dawn?"

"Not once in all those months, my small friend," Guido replied sadly.

Francisco winked at Pornada. Should he tell Guido what he knew?

"Enough of my troubles," Guido said. "Tell me how you've been."

"We have been fine, mostly because of Francisco. He has worked like a man in his boy's way, helping us get through the winter," Papa said.

"No school?" Guido asked, alarmed.

"School too," Papa told him. "Along with school, he has painted and sold many of his paintings."

"Such a young artist," Guido said. "How is your painting going?"

Instead of answering, Francisco went to the shelf where he kept his new paintings. Carefully he brought one to the table. Guido looked at it. Then he leaned nearer as if to see better. His eyes opened wide and he seemed almost frightened.

"Francisco?" he asked in a frightened voice.
Francisco nodded. "What do you think?"

"This is true?" Guido asked. "This is not a
dream you had, but something you saw?"

Papa and Mama came from their places to stare
over Guido's shoulder. Even little Josi leaned
against Guido's knee for a better look.

"It is a nice painting," Papa said in a puzzled
voice. "It is a tree whose leaves have left for the
winter, a hillside, and some stones."

"And mist!" Guido cried excitedly. "Mist that
breathes from the rock! Show this place to me,
Francisco, and let us dig!"

"Pornada will lead us there," Francisco
laughed. "It is his favorite place. He would lead
me there each dawn if I would let him."

Francisco and Josi were sent to bed. The night seemed to pass slowly for Francisco. When he dreamed, his head was bright with the tales that Guido had told. In his dreams, he saw the pale mists of that rocky place.

Just before dawn, Francisco, Pornada, and Guido left. They climbed up the rocky hillside. Sleepy birds moved in the trees about them.

Then they were there. The three of them stood quietly and watched the sun come up. From the rock beneath one tree, they saw a small mist rise.

Guido started to dig. After a while, he knelt down, giving a cry of such gladness that Pornada squealed with joy, too.

"It is not very pretty," Francisco said. He and Pornada stared at the huge rock in Guido's hand.

"Wait until it has been cleaned, my friend," Guido replied.

Guido put the jade into a big brown bag and carried it over his shoulder. Dawn turned to day as they made their way down the mountain. He sang loudly as they walked down the path and into the house. Mama and Papa were getting ready for their day's work.

"My hands are not empty now," Guido roared. "Artists and dreamers—they are the real gem finders."

"I am so happy for you," Mama said, with her slow smile. "You will be as rich as you are happy."

"We will all be rich," he told her. "Half of this belongs to my friend here." He put a hand on Francisco's shoulder.

"It was Pornada," Francisco said.

"Pornada indeed. This is then the richest pig in all Mexico!"

1. What was the old Mexican legend that Guido believed?

2. How did Pornada help to prove the legend?

3. Why was Guido excited when he saw Francisco's painting?

4. Do you think Guido was a good man? Why?

5. On page 101, what told you that Francisco knew something important about the legend?

Apply the Skills

Find two details in the story that support the following statement:

Francisco and his family thought of Guido as a close friend.

Prewrite

Think about Francisco, his pet pig, and his friend Guido. What might you take with you if you and Guido went to hunt for jade? If you had a pet pig like Pornada, how would you take care of it?

Compose

Choose one of the activities below.

1. Imagine that Guido has asked you to go with him to hunt for jade. Write a paragraph that describes the things you and Guido will need to take on your trip.

2. Write a paragraph telling what you would do if you had a pet pig. Where would you keep it? What would it eat? What games would you play with your pig?

Revise

Check your work to make sure that you have written a good descriptive paragraph. Make any changes that are needed.

Encyclopedia

When you want to find information on a topic, one place to look is an encyclopedia. An **encyclopedia** is a set of books that contains hundreds of articles about many topics. Each book in the set is called a **volume.**

Look at the encyclopedia shown below. Notice that each volume has a letter or letters on it. The books in the set are arranged in alphabetical order.

ENCYCLOPEDIA	ENCYCLOPEDIA	ENCYCLOPEDIA	ENCYCLOPEDIA	ENCYCLOPEDIA	ENCYCLOPEDIA	ENCYCLOPEDIA	ENCYCLOPEDIA	ENCYCLOPEDIA	ENCYCLOPEDIA	ENCYCLOPEDIA	ENCYCLOPEDIA	ENCYCLOPEDIA	ENCYCLOPEDIA	ENCYCLOPEDIA	ENCYCLOPEDIA	ENCYCLOPEDIA	ENCYCLOPEDIA	ENCYCLOPEDIA	ENCYCLOPEDIA	ENCYCLOPEDIA
A	B	C-Ch.	Ci-Cz	D	E	H	I	J-K	L	M	N-O	P	Q-R	S-Sn	So-Sz	T	U-V	W-X Y-Z	Resear Guide Inde.
1	2	3	4	5	6	9	10	11	12	13	14	15	16	17	18	19	20	21	22

Finding Information in an Encyclopedia

The topics within each volume are also arranged in alphabetical order. The volume marked "A" contains articles on any topic that begins with the letter *a*. In the "A" volume, you could find information about Africa, the Alamo, or ants.

Topics having more than one word are alphabetized by the first word. For example, if you wanted to find information about New York, you would look in the "N" volume. Where would you look to find information about the Rocky Mountains? Yes, you would look in the "R" volume.

If you want to find information about a person, use the first letter of the person's last name. You would find an article about Claude Monet in the "M" volume of the encyclopedia, under "Monet." Where would you find an article about Benjamin Franklin? Yes, you would find it in the "F" volume, under "Franklin."

Suppose you want to find out where sequoia trees grow. You would first look in the "S" volume under "sequoia" because that is the name of the special tree that interests you. If you can't find the information there, look in the "T" volume under "tree."

Suppose you wanted to find out about African and Indian elephants. Would you look up "Africa," "India," or "elephants"? Since the topic is elephants, you would go to the "E" volume.

Using the Encyclopedia

Look at the picture of the encyclopedia on page 108. Tell the letter of the volume you would use to find information on each of these topics:

1. Alexander Calder
2. legends
3. New Mexico
4. jade
5. South America
6. pearls
7. Betsy Ross
8. George Washington
9. corn oil
10. pine trees

Suppose you have been asked to report to your class about a gem and you have picked jade as your topic. You already know how to spell and say the word. You know from the story "Pornada" that jade is a gem. To find out where jade is found, what it looks like, how it is used, and other interesting facts about jade, you could use the encyclopedia.

In the "J" volume of the encyclopedia, you find that there are other topics that begin with the letters *ja*. How would you find *jade*? Yes, to find *jade,* you have to go to the third letter of the word *jade,* the letter *d*. Now you can begin reading about jade.

Encyclopedia Brown is known as a good detective. How does he solve this case?

The Case of the Cave Drawings

adapted from the story by Donald J. Sobol

Elmer Evans came into the Brown Detective Agency.

"You look worried," Encyclopedia told him. "Is something wrong?"

"Plenty," answered Elmer. "It's that Wilford Wiggins."

Wilford Wiggins was a high school boy with lots of get-rich-quick ideas.

"What's Wilford up to now?" Encyclopedia asked.

"Down to," corrected Elmer. "He climbed down that hole into the old bear cave the other day."

"Good grief!" exclaimed Encyclopedia. "All kids are supposed to stay away from that bear cave. The hole could be dangerous."

"Wilford has called a secret meeting for five o'clock at the cave," said Elmer. "He's going to tell all the kids what he found in the hole. He says he'll make us all rich."

"Wilford didn't ask me to the meeting," said Encyclopedia.

"I bet he's still mad at you," said Elmer. "He'll never forget how you spoiled his sale of Hercules Strength Tonic last month."

"That stuff was nothing but colored water!" exclaimed Encyclopedia. "I think I'll go to the meeting with you."

The bear cave was a mile outside the town line. When Encyclopedia and Elmer got to the bear cave, a crowd of boys and girls had already gathered outside the cave to hear Wilford.

Wilford raised his hands and called for quiet.

"Do you kids know what's inside this cave?" he asked.

"Sure we know," said Bugs Meany. "There's a lot of rock and a hole in the floor that goes down to China."

Wilford laughed.

"You want to know what I found at the bottom of that hole?" cried Wilford. "Another cave, even bigger than the one on top. On the walls were drawings—done by cave people!"

A thrill of excitement ran through the children.

"We'll keep this a secret, okay?" said Wilford. "If some smart grown-ups hear what's down in that hole, they'll buy this land in a hurry. They'll make a lot of money by charging people three dollars a ticket to see those cave drawings!"

The children nodded. There was a fortune in it!

"I can rent this land," said Wilford, "but I need a little more money. Then I can dig an opening to give people a better way to get into the lower cave."

"I knew you'd ask us for money," said Rocky Graham. He was a member of the Tigers, a club for tough older boys.

"Get lost, kid," said Wilford. To all the others he said, "I'm going to let each and every one of you buy a piece of this business for five dollars. We'll all make a fortune."

"How do we know that those walls have cave drawings on them?" asked Benny Breslin.

"After I found those cave drawings, I went home and got my camera," said Wilford. "I took pictures with a flash."

He passed out three photographs. The first was of a wooly rhinoceros. The second was of cave people attacking a dinosaur. The third was of a charging mammoth.

"There's the proof!" shouted Wilford. "For five dollars you'll all get a share of every ticket sold. So go home and get your money, but don't breathe a word of this to anyone!"

"Maybe I spoke too quickly, Wilford," Rocky Graham said. "I'm sorry. I've got ten dollars saved. Can I buy two shares?"

"Sure, sure, kid," said Wilford. "I don't have the heart to keep anybody from a really big money-making deal like this."

Rocky and the other Tigers raced for their bikes. They talked about using the club's money to buy all the shares themselves.

Encyclopedia watched the Tigers pedal away. Then he told the rest of the children to hold onto their money.

"No cave person drew those pictures," he said.

How did Encyclopedia know? Turn the next page upside down to find out.

Solution to ''The Case of the Cave Drawings''

Encyclopedia knew that Wilford Wiggins had drawn the cave pictures himself and then had photographed them.

One of the photographs that Wilford passed out showed a drawing of ''cave people attacking a dinosaur.'' That was Wilford's mistake! Since it is unlikely that the cave artists even knew about dinosaurs, they could not have known what a dinosaur looked like.

Because of Encyclopedia's sharp eye, Wilford went out of the cave business!

1. How did Encyclopedia Brown become interested in the case?

2. What clue helped Encyclopedia Brown solve the case?

3. Why did Encyclopedia Brown stop the kids from giving Wilford their money?

4. Do you think Wilford was a nice person? Why?

5. On page 116, what sentence told you that the Tigers thought only about themselves?

If the children in "The Case of the Cave Drawings" had read about dinosaurs in the encyclopedia, they would have known Wilford was trying to trick them. If they were to look up the list of things below, in which volumes of the encyclopedia on page 108 should they look?

1. wooly rhinoceros   2. mammoth

Prewrite

Long ago, people may have used pictures to write stories. Think about how you might write a story using just pictures. What kinds of pictures would you use? For example, these pictures could stand for a person, mountains, a river, and a tree:

Compose

Write a story just using pictures. Under your story, put a key that will help the reader know what word each picture stands for. Then write the story using words.

Revise

Check your work by having classmates read your picture story. If they cannot understand what you have said or drawn, revise your work.

Comparisons and Contrasts

Look at the two pictures. How are the shoes alike? Both are running shoes. How are they different? One shoe is larger than the other. One shoe is red, and the other is blue.

When we say how things are alike, we **compare** them. When we say how things are different, we **contrast** them.

Read the three groups of sentences below. Each group of sentences tells about Bob and Mike. Which group helps you know the most about Bob and Mike?

1. Bob likes to go to the movies. Mike likes to go to the movies, too.
2. Mike likes scary movies. Bob likes funny movies.
3. Bob and Mike like to go to the movies. Bob likes scary movies, but Mike likes funny ones.

120

The last group of sentences compares and contrasts the boys. This group of sentences helps you know Bob and Mike better.

Read the paragraph below. See how this writer compares and contrasts artists.

Artists work with paint, brushes, and canvas. Some artists use bright colors. Others use dark colors. Some artists paint people; others paint things. No matter what colors artists use or what they paint, artists are expressing themselves through their work.

How are artists alike? How are they different? The chart below will show you this information.

COMPARE (alike)
work with paint, brushes, canvas express themselves in work
CONTRAST (different)
bright colors   paint people dark colors   paint things

As you read, be sure to look for comparisons and contrasts. These comparisons and contrasts will give you clearer pictures of people and places.

Johnny has a problem. How does his sister Kate help him solve his problem?

The Cave

by Eleanor Clymer

This story is taken from a chapter of *The Spider, the Cave and the Pottery Bowl.* Kate and her younger brother Johnny spend each summer with their grandmother, who lives on a mesa.

Each year, Kate helps Grandmother make pottery, but this year there is no more clay. While Kate is holding a bowl which had belonged to the Old Ones — their Indian ancestors — Johnny bumps her arm. The bowl falls to the floor and smashes. Johnny feels very bad about this and goes to search for another bowl. As this story begins, Kate is going to look for Johnny.

"Grandmother," I said, "did you see Johnny this morning?" Grandmother said she hadn't seen him. I thought that since Johnny had broken the old bowl, he might have run away. Then I said to Grandmother, "I will see if I can find him."

She nodded and said, "He is troubled about the bowl. Tell him it does not matter. I am not angry."

I wrapped some food in a cloth. I put it in a basket and took a bottle of water. Then I started out.

It was lovely on the mesa early in the morning. The air was cool and fresh. When the sun came up, it made the houses look as if they were painted with light red paint.

From where I stood, I could see far out over the desert. The mesa stretched out for miles. Many kinds of desert plants grew on it.

I started to walk away from the village. I saw where twigs and leaves had been broken. I thought that must be the way Johnny had gone.

The valleys in the mesa were like big cracks in a table top. Some of those valleys were wide and had good soil for planting corn. We called them washes, because when there was a thunderstorm, the water washed down them like a flood. People put little fences around the plants so they wouldn't be washed away.

I looked up at the sky and thought, "I'm glad it's not going to rain today"—though we had been hoping for rain because it was so dry. But there were only white clouds in the blue sky, the fluffy kind that never do anything.

I was coming to one of those washes. The path led down the slope to cornfields at the bottom. I was getting very hot. The sun beat down on my head, and I wished that I had a hat. I took a drink of water. I was glad I had it.

Then I was ready to start down into the valley. It wasn't steep like the edge of the mesa, but it was pretty far down. I thought, "How do I know Johnny is down there?" I squinted my eyes. Yes, down in the valley I saw a boy on a burro. They looked very tiny. I yelled, "Johnny!" But of course he couldn't hear. So I started down.

The ground had a lot of loose sand and stones. I slid part way down, holding on to bushes as I went. At last I got to the bottom. Then I had to walk around a cornfield. I noticed that the corn looked thin. There hadn't been enough water.

Farther down the wash were some more fields. I saw people who were bent over and digging in the fields. I was getting tired and thought, "Why am I hurrying? Johnny knows the way back, and besides, he has the burro."

Then I squinted up at the sky, and I saw that there was good reason to hurry. Instead of the fluffy white clouds, all of a sudden there were thunderclouds. They were very tall gray clouds standing like mountains in the west.

The sun was still bright. As long as the clouds did not cover the sun, I did not feel frightened, but they were moving. In the desert a storm can come up in a few minutes. I began to run and to shout, "Johnny!"

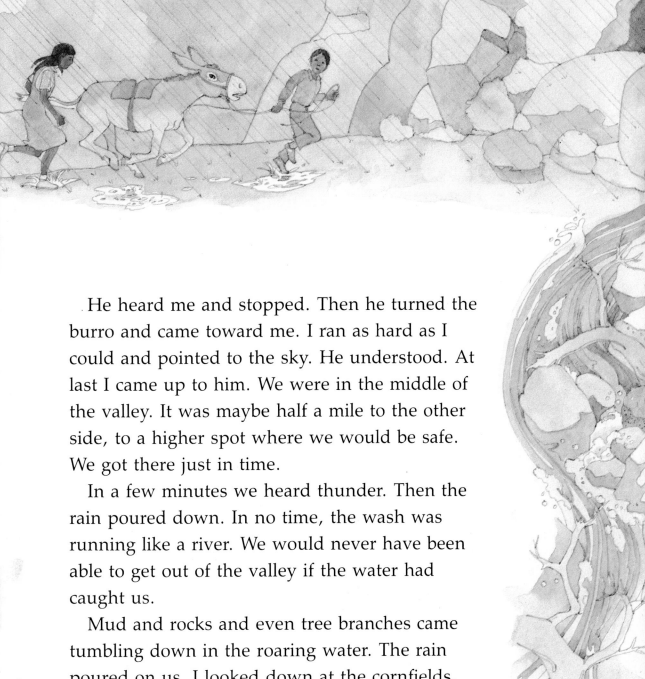

He heard me and stopped. Then he turned the burro and came toward me. I ran as hard as I could and pointed to the sky. He understood. At last I came up to him. We were in the middle of the valley. It was maybe half a mile to the other side, to a higher spot where we would be safe. We got there just in time.

In a few minutes we heard thunder. Then the rain poured down. In no time, the wash was running like a river. We would never have been able to get out of the valley if the water had caught us.

Mud and rocks and even tree branches came tumbling down in the roaring water. The rain poured on us. I looked down at the cornfields. The people were running up the bank to get away from the flood. I looked to see what Johnny was doing, but he was not beside me. Then I heard Johnny yell, "Come up here!"

He had found a cave, really an overhanging arch in the rock. Johnny was standing there out of the rain. I pulled the burro and went up there, too. We sat down and watched the rain fall. We sat for a long time. Finally I asked, "Where were you going?"

He said, "I was sorry I broke Grandmother's bowl. I wanted to find another one in the place where our ancestors lived. I didn't know how far it would be, so I took the burro."

I said, "Where were you going to look? I don't see any ruins around here."

We stood up and looked at the rock shelter we were in. At the back, under one end of the arch, there was a crack. It was really a hole in the rock, partly filled with stones and sand. We noticed that a thin stream of water ran out of it.

"Let's go in," Johnny said. "It looks like a deep hole. Maybe there are some ruins inside."

I shouted to Johnny, "Don't go in!" It was too late, however. He was inside the hole. I felt frightened, but I could not let him go in there alone. I tied the burro to a bush and crawled in after Johnny.

It was pretty dark inside. When my eyes got used to the darkness, I saw Johnny at the back of the cave.

"Did you find anything?" I asked.

"Yes," said Johnny. "An old basket, and a stick."

I went over to the basket. I dragged it closer to the light and looked inside.

Johnny said, "It's just a lot of dirt. I wanted to find pottery."

I said, "Johnny, you did!"

He thought I was joking. He said, "It's only sand."

I said, "It's not sand. It's clay! There's clay in this cave. Look! It's the same kind of clay that Grandmother uses to make pottery! You didn't find an old bowl, you found something better! Now we will be able to make our own bowls again with Grandmother."

1. What was Johnny's problem?

2. How did Kate help Johnny?

3. Why was the old basket that Johnny found in the cave important?

4. Would you like to have Kate for a sister or friend? Why?

5. How do you know that Grandmother was not upset about the broken bowl?

When things are alike, we compare them. When they are different, we contrast them. Are the following sentences from "The Cave" comparisons or contrasts?

1. Both Kate and her grandmother make pottery.

2. Valleys in a mesa are like cracks on a table.

3. Instead of fluffy, white clouds, Kate saw that there were thunderclouds.

Prewrite

In the story, Johnny caused Kate to drop and break a pottery bowl. How did Johnny feel after the bowl broke? How did Johnny try to solve his problem?

Compose

Read the incomplete story below. Finish it by writing an ending that shows how Jenny will solve the problem.

Jenny's friend, Mrs. Hill, loved her garden. She spent many hours working there. One day, Jenny's puppy ran into the garden and dug up most of the flowers.

"Oh, no!" Jenny cried. "How can I face Mrs. Hill? It took her so long to make this garden beautiful. What will I do?"

Revise

Read your completed story. Make sure you have written an ending that tells how Jenny solved her problem. Revise your work if corrections are needed.

Corn-Grinding Song
A poem of the Zuñi Indians

Lovely! See the cloud, the cloud appear!
Lovely! See the rain, the rain draw near!
    Who spoke?
Twas the little corn-ear
High on the tip of the stalk
Saying while it looked at me
    Talking aloft there—
"Ah, perchance the floods
    Hither moving—
Ah, may the floods come this way!"

Plants and animals can be found in a desert. How are they able to survive?

The Desert: What Lives There

by Andrew Bronin

The desert is a place that gets very little rainfall. The ground is often sandy and rocky. When the sun beats down, the sand and rocks grow hot and dry. It is hard to imagine that a place like this is full of living things.

All living things need food, shelter, and some kind of protection to survive. Some plants and animals make their homes in the desert because they have found these things there.

A cactus plant is at home in the desert. The cactus has a special way of getting water in the dry desert soil. It spreads its roots out close to the top of the ground. When rain comes, the cactus roots soak up all the water they can.

Once a cactus plant gets water, it saves the water for the dry days ahead. A cactus stores up enough water in one rainstorm to last a long time.

The desert tortoise is also at home in the desert. It gets most of the water it needs from the plants it eats, but it drinks water, too. When it rains, the tortoise drinks all the water it can. It stores the extra water under its shell. It can live for months without taking another drink.

The kangaroo rat is another animal at home in the dry desert. It can make water from the dry seeds that it eats. From the seeds, it gets what is needed to make water inside itself. It never has to take a drink of water in its life.

The cactus, the tortoise, and the kangaroo rat can live in the desert because they know how to get water. However, water is not the only thing that plants and animals need to survive in the desert. They also need protection.

The kangaroo rat can protect itself. When a snake or a fox tries to catch it, the kangaroo rat jumps high into the air, like a kangaroo. The kangaroo rat can also kick sand into its enemy's face. All the snake or fox gets is a mouthful of sand!

The tortoise can also protect itself. It just pulls its legs and head into its tough shell. Not even the strongest animal can bite through a tortoise shell.

The cactus protects itself, too. It has sharp spines all over its stem. Animals would eat the juicy cactus if it didn't have spines. Because the spines are so sharp, most animals won't touch the cactus.

Some plants and animals are at home in the desert because they get along well with each other.

The gila woodpecker is very much at home with the cactus. Its enemies would love to eat the gila woodpecker, but it has found a way to keep safe. The gila woodpecker uses the cactus' spines for protection. It pecks a hole high in the tallest cactus. There it builds a nest. Its enemies can't climb the cactus to get it.

The elf owl doesn't know how to peck a hole in the cactus, but it does the next best thing. It waits until a gila woodpecker leaves its nest. Then it moves in. The elf owl needs the gila woodpecker—just as the gila woodpecker needs the cactus.

The sun makes the desert sand very hot. Many desert animals don't like the heat, but there are no caves to hide in and no trees to curl up under. These desert animals spend their days underground, away from the hot sun.

The pack rat lives underground. It digs a hole and fills it with odds and ends that it finds in the desert. In a pack rat's hole you might find anything from a feather to a piece of an old car.

The badger lives underground, too. It digs a hole and spends the day there. The badger comes out at night when it's cooler and goes hunting for food.

Some animals can't dig their own holes. They have learned to let other animals dig for them. The desert cottontail is like the elf owl. Since the desert cottontail can't dig its own holes, it moves into holes that other animals have left.

If you were alone on the desert, do you think
you could survive? You could, if you learned
from the plants and animals that live there.

You know that you could get water from the
cactus. You could also take shelter underground.
For you, however, the desert would always be
a strange place. For the plants and animals that
get along well together in the desert, the desert
is not a strange place at all. It is home.

1. How are some plants and animals able to survive in the desert?

2. How do the cactus, desert tortoise, and kangaroo rat protect themselves?

3. How do some desert plants and animals get along well together?

4. What is the most interesting fact you learned from this article?

5. How do you know that the author thinks people would not like living in the desert?

We compare and contrast things to see how they are alike and how they are different. Think about the plants and animals in "The Desert." Then answer the following questions.

1. How are the cactus and the tortoise alike?

2. How are the gila woodpecker and the elf owl different?

Prewrite

In the selection, you were asked if you could survive in the desert. Imagine that you are moving to the desert. What would you need? How would your life change?

Compose

Choose one of the activities below.

1. Pretend that you have just moved to the desert. Write a story about your first day there. Use words like *first, next,* and *last* to show the order in which things happened. Tell what you like about the desert, how it is different from your real home, and what problems you might face.

2. Pretend that you are camping in the desert, and you brought only five things with you. Write a paragraph that tells what you brought to help you survive. How will these things help you?

Revise

Check your work carefully. Revise your work if you have not answered each question.

Thinking About "Landscapes"

In this unit, you learned that people look at landscapes in different ways. Some people use landscapes as settings for their paintings. Others may find something new or surprising in their landscapes. Did you notice that the way some people think about their landscapes may also change?

Eleanor's landscape became more pleasing to her when she found out that she could draw. The landscapes that Francisco painted helped to prove an old Mexican legend. Monet painted landscapes as his life's work. How did the author of "The Desert: What Lives There" use comparison and contrast to help you understand what a desert landscape is like?

As you read other stories, look for the landscape that may play an important part in a character's life. Look to see if any characters look at their landscapes in a new way. Look for the comparisons and contrasts among the different landscapes.

1. Landscapes are all that you see around you. Think about the landscapes painted by Monet and those painted by Francisco. How are they alike? How are they different?

2. Compare and contrast the surprise that Encyclopedia Brown found in a cave with the surprise that Kate and Johnny found.

3. In which stories did a drawing or painting of a landscape help to solve a problem? How?

4. Which stories had landscapes that could be hard or dangerous to live in?

5. If you were an artist, which landscape that you read about would you most like to paint? Why?

Read on Your Own

Desert Voices by Byrd Baylor. Scribner's. Desert animals describe the beauty of the desert.

The Skate Patrol Rides Again by Eve Bunting. Whitman. Two young detectives figure out who has been stealing pets from their apartment building.

The Living World: Deserts by Dr. Clive Catchpole. Dutton. This book tells about the desert and the plants and animals that live there.

The Spider, the Cave and the Pottery Bowl by Eleanor Clymer. Atheneum. "The Cave" was taken from a chapter in this book. Read the rest of the book to find out more about Kate, Johnny, and their grandmother.

Liang and the Magic Paintbrush by Demi. Holt. This tale is about a boy and a magic paintbrush. He uses it to help others, until a greedy emperor finds out about it.

Lizard Lying in the Sun by Bernice Freschet. Scribner's. This nature story tells how a lizard escapes from an eagle.

The Girl Who Loved Wild Horses by Paul Goble. Bradbury. An American Indian girl lives among a herd of wild horses.

Star Boy by Paul Goble. Bradbury. Star Boy goes to live in the sky in this American Indian legend.

Deserts by Elsa Posell. Childrens Press. Desert plants and animals are described in this book.

Popcorn by Millicent E. Selsam. Morrow. This book describes the kind of corn used to make popcorn and tells how you can grow your own popcorn plant.

Pornada by Mary Francis Shura. Atheneum. The story you read was taken from two chapters in this book. Read the rest of the book to find out more about Francisco and Pornada.

Encyclopedia Brown Keeps the Peace by Donald J. Sobol. Dutton. "The Case of the Cave Drawings" is one of ten mysteries in this book. Try solving the others—the answers are not given until the end of the book.

Unit 3

Applause

Think about the different times you have heard applause. Have you ever heard people clapping their hands after seeing a funny play or when a home run was hit in a baseball game?

Applause is just one way of telling someone that you are pleased with what he or she did. Telling that person in words is another way. Sometimes the look on your face is enough to show how you feel. What are some other ways to share your feelings or to praise someone?

In "Applause," you will meet characters who express themselves in different ways. As you read the stories in this unit, think about how the characters share their good feelings with others.

How do the members of the family in this story talk to each other? What are "words in our hands"?

Words in Our Hands

by Ada B. Litchfield

My name is Michael Turner. I am nine years old. I have two sisters, Gina and Diane, a dog named Polly, and two parents who can't hear me when I talk. They never have heard me. You see, my mom and dad were born deaf.

My parents never heard any sounds at all when they were babies. Some people think deaf people can't learn to talk. That's not true.

My mother and father went to a school for deaf children when they were growing up. That's where they learned to talk. They learned by placing their fingers on their teacher's throat and feeling how words felt in her voice box as she said them. They learned how words looked by watching her face, especially her lips, as she spoke. It's hard to learn to say words that way, but my parents did learn to talk.

They don't talk much now, but they can talk. Since they have never heard other people talking or even their own voices, they don't know how voices sound. It's not always easy to tell what they are saying, but Gina, Diane, and I can understand them.

When we communicate with our parents, most of the time we talk with our hands as well as with our mouths. One way to communicate with your hands is to learn a special alphabet so you can spell words with your fingers. This is called finger spelling.

Another way to communicate with your hands is to use sign language. Learning to sign is like learning a whole new language. You have to learn the same signs that other people have learned so that you can be understood. Most of the time one sign stands for one word, but sometimes it can stand for more than one word. Once you have learned sign language, it is much faster to use than finger spelling.

Gina, Diane, and I are learning new signs all the time. Mother and Father learned sign language when they were little. They taught us signs when we were babies, just as hearing parents teach their children words. Our grandparents, friends, and neighbors helped us learn to talk.

Sometimes my mother and father understand
what people are saying by reading their lips.
That's another thing my parents learned at their
school—lipreading.

Reading lips is hard. Some people don't move
their lips much when they talk. Some people hide
their mouths with their hands. Besides, many
words look alike when you say them. Look in the
mirror and say "pin" and "bin," "hill" and "ill." See
what I mean?

The way we move our bodies and the way our
faces look when we talk help our parents read our
lips. Most of the time we talk to them with our
hands. Our grandmother says we have words in
our hands.

My parents have some interesting things to help them. In our house, when the telephone or doorbell rings, lights flash on and off. We also have a special machine attached to our phone. It types the messages onto paper. Then my parents can type messages back.

Of course, the people calling us must have the same kind of machine attached to their telephones, and not very many people do. That means that many times we have to talk on the telephone for our parents.

Some deaf people have a hearing ear dog to help them. Our dog, Polly, isn't a trained hearing ear dog, but she can do many things a hearing ear dog does.

Polly can get my parents up by tugging at their covers if the flashing-light alarm doesn't wake them. If the doorbell rings, Polly will run back and forth to let my mom and dad know someone is at the door.

We are a happy family. At least we were until about six months ago. Then the company where my father has always worked moved to a new town, one hundred miles away.

It took a long time to get used to our new town. In our old town, nobody stared when they saw us talking with our hands. In the new town, people did stare. They pretended they didn't see us, but I knew they were looking.

One day Gina's favorite teacher gave her a note to take home asking for our family to go to a play by the National Theater of the Deaf. Gina said that the play would be in sign language. Who would understand it better than our parents?

The night of the play, the big hall was filled with people. Just inside the door, my mother signed to me, "Where will we sit?"

To our surprise, a man stood up and signed, "There are five seats over here."

153

We couldn't believe it. He was talking to us in sign language! All around us, the people in the audience were talking with their hands.

We learned from the program that some of the actors were deaf and some could hear. During the play, the hearing actors and some of the deaf actors would speak. All of the actors would sign, sometimes for themselves and sometimes for each other. Everyone in the audience would be able to understand what was going on in the play.

I was proud of my parents. They were smiling, and their fingers were flying as fast as anyone's. For the first time in months, they seemed to feel at home.

Then we had another surprise. Gina's teacher came over to us. She talked very slowly and very carefully so my parents could read her lips. Then she signed with her hands!

Gina was excited. Her favorite teacher, who wasn't deaf, had words in her hands, too. We were learning there were many friendly people in our new town who could talk with our parents. This place wasn't going to be so bad, after all.

After the play, we went backstage to meet the people in the acting company. The deaf actors talked with people who knew sign language. The hearing actors helped the other people understand what was being said.

I think some of the hearing people around us were learning something, too. Being deaf doesn't mean a person can't hear or talk. If they have to, people can hear with their eyes and talk with their hands.

1. What does "words in our hands" mean?

2. What are three ways in which Michael communicates with his parents?

3. How did Gina's favorite teacher help the Turner family?

4. Do you think the Turner family is happier in their new home now? Why?

5. What are two things the author says a hearing ear dog can do?

Apply

the

Skills

An *effect* is something that happens, and a *cause* is the reason that it happens. Each incomplete sentence below states an effect in the story. On another sheet of paper, complete each sentence with the cause.

1. Michael's parents don't know how voices sound because ▬▬▬.

2. In Michael's house, a light flashes when the doorbell rings because ▬▬▬.

Prewrite

Communication means expressing ideas to others. You just read about the Turner family and how they learned to communicate. Think about ways you could communicate with others if you could not talk or if others could not hear you.

Compose

Choose one of the activities below.

1. Write a paragraph explaining this sentence: "If they have to, people can hear with their eyes and talk with their hands."

2. Write a letter to a friend explaining three ways in which the Turner family's life is different from yours. Remember to follow the rules of writing a friendly letter.

Revise

Read your paragraph or letter. Did you follow the directions given? Will your paragraph or letter make sense to someone reading it? If not, revise your work.

Shh

by Eve Merriam

If I covered up my ears
I couldn't hear
car horns honk
garbage cans clang
screen doors bang
toasters tick
or crickets crick

or telephones ring
or foghorns hoot
or grease spatter
or fire crackle
and sigh to ash

or paper crumble
or thunder crash
or the squeak of a rocker
or the shout of a crowd
or the crack of a nut
or a motorboat's putt.

But
could I hear a feather
or a snowflake
or a cloud?

This is an interview with an actor from a theater of the deaf. How do these actors communicate?

Listen With Your Eyes

by Janice Cooper

The circus is coming to town! Soon you will hear loud happy music, and lions roaring, and people laughing. You will hear the booming voice of the ringmaster telling about each act.

But what if you couldn't hear these sounds? What if you couldn't hear at all?

160

In the following interview, actors from a theater of the deaf in Cleveland, Ohio, tell about their special circus of signs. Come along with the Fairmount Theater of the Deaf as they present the "Smircus"!

Question: What is the Smircus?

Answer: The Smircus is one of the plays performed by the Fairmount Theater of the Deaf. The play used to be called "Circus of Signs." It was thought up by two of our actors, Adrian Blue and Debbie Taylor. Adrian, who is deaf, had the idea for a circus that was performed using different kinds of communication. We use mostly sign language and pantomime in the Smircus. Very few words are spoken in our show.

Question: Then how do hearing people understand what is happening in the Smircus?

Answer: Hearing people may be able to understand some of the signs because they look like what they mean. But everyone can understand pantomime.

Question: Are pantomime and sign language alike?

Answer: Yes, but they have one big difference. Pantomime is a special form of art, while sign language is for everyday communication.

Question: Do you have real circus acts in the
Smircus?

Answer: Yes! We have a juggler, a tightrope walker,
and a snake charmer. We even have trained
bears that roller-skate!

Question: It sounds as if the Smircus is quite a show! Do you perform it in many different places?

Answer: We perform in schools and in theaters. We have also performed on television. Our first television show was about "Beauty and the Beast." We have taken the Smircus with us to perform in several different countries, too. In one of the countries we visited, Smircus won an award as the show that the audience liked best.

Question: What else does the Fairmount Theater of the Deaf do?

Answer: This year we are giving a lot of school workshops. We teach children a little about acting. We help them learn pantomime, too.

Question: Do you work only with deaf children?

Answer: No, but since we are a deaf theater, we
especially try to help children who have hearing
problems. One of our dreams is to make videotapes
to help teach deaf children. We want deaf
children to understand that being deaf is not a
bad thing. It's important that deaf children know
that they can do everything that hearing people
can do, except hear. We try to show deaf people
that there are ways to communicate without
spoken words. Using sign language puts words
in their hands. Deaf people learn how to listen
with their eyes.

1. How do the actors in a theater of the deaf communicate?

2. What does "listen with your eyes" mean?

3. What do the actors want deaf children to understand?

4. Would you like to go to the Smircus? Why?

5. How do you know that people like the Smircus?

"Listen With Your Eyes" is an interview. The actor's own words tell what the theater group does. Read the following sentences. Which one would be in a story? Which one would be in an interview?

1. Answer: We use mostly sign language and pantomime in the Smircus.

2. He said, "We use mostly sign language and pantomime in the Smircus."

Prewrite

Most people can see and hear. Imagine all the sights and sounds of a circus. Think about the animal acts and the clowns.

Compose

Choose one of the activities below.

1. Imagine that you can hear, but not see. Write a paragraph describing four things you might hear at a circus. Remember, you must use only your hearing to describe the circus.

2. Pretend that you are at the circus. You can see, but not hear. Write a paragraph describing four things you might see. Remember, you must use only your sight to describe the circus.

Revise

Read your paragraph. Check to be sure you have used only sight or only sound in your description. Revise your work if necessary.

Alphabet Stew

by Jack Prelutsky

Words can be stuffy, as sticky as glue,
but words can be tutored to tickle you too,
to rumble and tumble and tingle and sing,
to buzz like a bumblebee, coil like a spring.

Juggle their letters and jumble their sounds,
swirl them in circles and stack them in mounds,
twist them and tease them and turn them about,
teach them to dance upside down, inside out.

Make mighty words whisper and tiny words roar
in ways no one ever had thought of before;
cook an improbable alphabet stew,
and words will reveal little secrets to you.

Context Clues

When you are reading, you may come to a word that you do not know. Sometimes the **context,** the other words in the sentence, will give you clues to the meaning of the word.

Read the following sentence. Look for clues in the sentence that will help you understand the meaning of the word *museum.*

Nancy and Ashley went to the *museum* to see the display of Monet's paintings.

What words in this sentence help you know the meaning of the word *museum*? The words *went to* give you a clue that a museum is a place. The words *see the display of Monet's paintings* help you know what kind of a place a museum is. The context of this sentence helps you know that a museum is a place to display paintings and other works of art.

Read the sentence at the top of page 171. Look for context clues to help you figure out the meaning of *visual arts.*

Tanya likes the visual arts—arts such as painting and film.

In this sentence the words *painting and film* tell you that the *visual arts* are forms of art that you can see.

Now read the following two sentences. Which sentence has context that helps you know the meaning of the word *videotape*?

1. Josh and Steve watched a *videotape* of the baseball game.
2. A *videotape* is a special kind of tape on which images and sounds are recorded to be played back at another time.

Sentence 2 tells you the meaning of the word *videotape*. However, the context in sentence 1 helps you know that a *videotape* is something that people can watch. Both sentences have contexts that help you understand the meaning of *videotape*.

When you come to a word whose meaning you do not know, look at the other words around it. Context may give you a clue to the meaning of the unknown word, as in sentence 1. Some context may tell you exactly what the word means, as in sentence 2.

Textbook Application: Context Clues in Social Studies

Read the following paragraphs from two social studies books. The sidenotes will show you how context clues help you understand the meaning of new words.

Communication is an important word. Look at the context for help. The next sentence tells you exactly what *communication* means.

The context of this paragraph tells you two ways that people communicate.

You use telephones, phonographs, radios, tape recorders, and television without thinking them strange. They are part of everyday life.

All of these things are forms of **communication.** Communication is the way people trade thoughts and information.

The first way people communicated was by talking. And it was the only way, for a very long time. Then about five thousand years ago, people found a way of writing things down. For the first time, words didn't float away as soon as they were spoken. A message marked in wet clay could be kept or even carried from one place to another.

—*City, Town, and Country,* Scott Foresman

Changes in Communication

People have always needed to communicate and share ideas. Long ago people had only a few ways to communicate. They could talk with each other or write letters. There were no radios, televisions, or telephones until people **invented** them. *Invent* means "to make something that no one else has ever made."

Some people have always searched for new and better ways to share information. Their inventions have changed the ways in which we communicate today.

—*Communities and Resources*, Silver Burdett

Invented is an important word. What does it mean?

As you read, you can probably figure out what new words mean by using context clues.

Hattie the Backstage Bat

story and pictures by Don Freeman

The backstage of a dark, empty theater is a lonely place. Only a bat would feel at home there. To a little bat named Hattie, this *was* home.

She had lived in the theater all her life. She had never seen a tree or a haunted house. Hattie's sky was the open space high above the stage.

Every night Hattie flew about for hours. She flew in and out of the ropes and between the stage curtains. When she was tired, Hattie landed in her favorite place and went to sleep.

The only person who knew about Hattie was Mr. Collins. He came to the theater every morning to sweep the floor and keep things neat.

There hadn't been a show in the old theater for quite a long time, but Mr. Collins was never lonely. He had Hattie to keep him company. Once he made Hattie a tiny hat out of odds and ends he found in an old trunk.

Each day at noon Mr. Collins shared his lunch with Hattie. Since Mr. Collins knew that bats like to eat flowers, he always brought Hattie a daisy.

While they ate, Hattie listened to Mr. Collins. He talked about the plays that had been on that stage.

One afternoon Mr. Collins had important news to tell Hattie. "Starting today, some actors will be coming here to rehearse for a new play," he said. "You'll have to stay out of sight. People get very frightened if they see a bat flying around."

Day after day, the actors came in and rehearsed their parts. Since this was a mystery play, the actors spoke their lines mostly in whispers. Soon they knew all their lines by heart. Day after day Hattie kept well out of sight. It was only late at night that she flew down to the stage to eat the delicious treats Mr. Collins had left for her.

One morning Hattie woke up to the sound of hammering. The scenery for the play was being set up on the stage. There below, Hattie saw not only a tree, but a three-story house that looked like it was haunted! The scenery was built to order for a bat!

Weeks went by. Finally there was the dress rehearsal. Hattie watched in surprise. An actor was wearing a long black cape. He looked like a huge bat! Then he began to climb in and out of the windows of the house.

"Why doesn't he fly the way I do?" Hattie said to herself. "I could show that actor how to act like a bat." Still, Hattie didn't move.

At last, it was the opening night. Everybody backstage was nervous and excited. Mr. Collins was the most nervous of all. Would Hattie stay out of sight on the most important night of all?

In the theater, the audience was beginning to settle into their seats. Since they had come to see a mystery play, they were ready to be frightened.

The lights went out and everyone was quiet. Slowly the curtain went up. The actor dressed as a bat entered. He tiptoed across the stage.

The audience groaned. They had seen plays about bat-people many times before. "I wanted to see a scary play," said one lady, sighing.

"So did I," whispered another. "How boring!"

There was one small bat in the theater who was not bored. "It's a great night for a bat like me!" thought Hattie. She could hold herself back no longer!

Spreading her wings wide, Hattie flew down through the open attic window. As she flew across the spotlight, she made a huge shadow that spread across the whole stage!

The men and women screamed! The audience became wild with fear when it saw that a real bat was flying above their heads. The screaming was just too much for Hattie. All at once, in plain sight, she flew back through the attic window.

The audience stood and cheered. "Bravo, bat!" they shouted. "Bravo!" Hattie had indeed saved the show.

So, of course, Hattie was asked to perform her wonderful flying act every night after that. She was a great star. Each night after the show, Mr. Collins proudly presented a delicious white rose to Hattie.

1. Who got the applause at the end of this story? Why?

2. Why did Mr. Collins give Hattie a white rose after each show?

3. How did Hattie save the show?

4. Do you think Mr. Collins was a nice man? Why?

5. When did you know that Hattie was not going to be able to stay out of sight?

Sentence context can help you understand new words. Which words in the following sentence pairs gives clues to the meaning of each underlined word?

1. Mr. Collins knew that bats like to eat flowers. Each day he brought Hattie a daisy.

2. The actors rehearsed their parts. They practiced until they knew their lines by heart.

Prewrite

Hattie the bat had always lived in the theater. She had never seen the outside world. Suppose that you could talk to Hattie. What would you tell her about the world outside the theater?

Compose

Pretend that Hattie has asked you about the outside world. Choose one of the places below, and write a descriptive paragraph which answers her questions. Include at least three sentences that tell Hattie why she would like that place.

1. A cave in the forest

2. A house high on a hill

Revise

After you have written your description, check your work to be sure you have listed three reasons why Hattie would like that place. Revise your work if changes are needed.

Schedules

Rita has many after-school activities. She has soccer practice, a 4-H meeting, a music lesson, and piano practice. Now Rita wants to join the Book Club, which meets on Tuesday.

Rita's mother suggested that Rita make a **schedule,** or plan, of her activities before she joins anything else. Her mother helped her make a schedule. Rita wrote the days of the week across the top of the schedule and listed after-school hours on the left side. Then she filled in the activities she already had. Rita's finished schedule looked like this:

	Monday	Tuesday	Wednesday	Thursday	Friday
3-4	Soccer Practice		4-H Club meeting	Soccer Practice	
4-5	Practice Piano	Music Lesson	Practice Piano	Practice Piano	Practice Piano
5-6	Set table and eat Dinner	—	—	—	→

When Rita looked at her schedule, she saw that she had one hour free on Tuesday and another hour free on Friday. The Book Club meets on Tuesday at three o'clock. Will Rita be able to join the Book Club? Since she is free on Tuesday at three o'clock, Rita decides to join the Book Club. Now how much free time will she have? When will that free time be?

Sometimes a schedule has already been made for you. One example of this is a TV schedule. A TV schedule tells you which programs are on and when each program starts and ends. If you can watch TV only from eight o'clock to nine o'clock each night, which program that lasts an hour can you watch?

Channels ❷WXYZ-TV ❹ KZKB-TV ❼WEDT-TV
T.V. Schedule

7:30		8:30	
❹	Baseball Game	❷	All About Bats
❼	Animals in Africa	9:00	
8:00		❷	Special News Report
❷	A Visit to the Museum	❼	Movie
❼	Mystery Theatre		

A schedule is a plan of things to be done or a list of times telling when things will happen. A schedule helped Rita plan her time. Using a schedule can help you plan your time.

How does Sammy find a way to be in the next family picture?

All Except Sammy

by Gladys Yessayan Cretan

A photographer from the newspaper comes to take a picture of Sammy Agabashian's musical family. While the picture is being taken, Sammy just sits and watches. He pretends he doesn't care. Sammy tries hard, but he can't play a musical instrument. He loves to play baseball. One day Sammy stops by the museum on his way to baseball practice. As part of their homework, everyone in Sammy's class has to find a painting to tell about in school. As the story begins, Sammy is walking around the museum, looking for a painting.

"There!" Sammy said. "There's a picture I could talk about." He stopped and looked for a long time at a painting of a soldier sitting tall on a proud black horse.

Across the quietness, a voice said, "Hi, Sammy!" Sammy turned to see his friend Jason standing in front of a large picture of the sea.

"Hi!" said Sammy. "Did you find your picture?"

"I guess I like this one," said Jason. "It looks like a big storm. What about you?"

"I'll tell about this one," Sammy said. "We had better go now. We're going to be late for the game, and they can't start it without us."

The next day Sammy told his class about the picture of the soldier and the horse he had seen at the museum. "That horse could run like the wind," Sammy said.

Jason looked puzzled. "How could you tell?"

"You could see it in the picture!" said Sammy. "I could tell that from the way the muscles were drawn, and from the proud way the horse held its head. We'll stop there after school on the way to the ball park. I'll show you."

Later, as they stood in front of the picture, Sammy said, "Look at the power in that horse. Look at those muscles. You mean to tell me that horse can't run?"

After a long look, Jason shook his head. "That's a lot to tell from a painting," he said.

Sammy nodded. "It's a lot for someone to show, with just a little paint. I'd like to learn how to do that."

As they left the museum, Sammy pointed to a sign near the door. It said there was a painting class for children on Saturday mornings.

"Look!" Sammy said. "That's for me."

They walked down the wide steps and then turned toward the ball field. Suddenly Jason thought of something.

"Hey!" he said. "Sammy! What about Saturday baseball practice?"

"I'll only be a little late," Sammy said. "I wouldn't miss practice."

"What about Tug Smith?" said Jason.

"We decided in the tryouts," said Sammy. "I play first base, and he's my substitute."

Across the field they could see Tug standing at first base like he owned it. Sammy and Jason walked up to him. "Hi," said Tug. "I'm playing first base today, since you're late."

"Listen," said Sammy. "I'm going to be late on Saturdays, too, because I have to take a class. You're my substitute, fair enough, but I was picked to play first base. I'll be here as fast as I can."

"There's no school on Saturday," said Tug.

"I know," said Sammy. "This is a special art class at the museum."

"Art?" laughed Tug.

"Listen," Sammy said. "Can you paint a horse that looks like it can really run? Can you use gray, orange, and white, and still make a cape that looks red?"

Tug shook his head. "I can't either," said Sammy, "but that's what I'm going to try to learn. So I'll be late on Saturdays. You can be my substitute till I get here."

So every Saturday, while Sammy's mama gave music lessons downstairs, his brother and sister practiced their instruments upstairs. His papa went to band practice. Sammy went to art class.

"What about the baseball team?" Papa asked as he walked one morning with Sammy toward the museum. "I get there a little late," Sammy said. "The fellows don't mind because I'm painting a poster to show when we're playing."

"They're lucky to have an artist on the team," said Papa. "Look at the trouble we have getting our program covers planned. Our posters for the front of the concert hall don't even look like musical posters. They look like circus posters! Well, here's the museum. Learn well!"

When Jason got to the museum to pick Sammy up, Sammy was sitting quietly in front of a picture of a little girl. "Studying something new?" asked Jason.

"Blue," said Sammy. "This week I'm studying blue. Look," he pointed, "look at that blue dress. It's part green and part black, but it all looks blue."

"That's a fact," said Jason. "I never saw it that way before." He picked up Sammy's mitt and gave it a punch. "We get to use the big field today," he said. "Can you play late?"

"Sure," said Sammy. "There's no use going home early today, anyway. There's a photographer coming to take a picture of the family."

"You're in the family," said Jason.

"I know," said Sammy, "but he only wants the musicians in the family—everyone but me."

"Never mind, Sammy," said Jason. "Maybe you can't play an instrument, but you sure can draw."

"That's true," said Sammy. "I can draw. I've been thinking. Why can't *I* make the program poster for their concert? I'll bet I could plan a good poster."

Sammy worked very hard for days and days. Sometimes he painted at the museum, and sometimes at home. One day Sammy's brother called, "Look! Look at Sammy's poster!"

His sister said, "This is better than any poster we've ever had." It was, too.

So the next time a photographer came, he put Sammy right in the middle of the family, holding his poster. When the picture of all the Agabashians was in the newspaper, they were called "an artistic family."

"Boy!" said Sammy. "Look at that! I finally got in the picture."

"Why not?" said his father. "Must everyone play an instrument? No. You are an artist—and a good one!"

"Not only that," said his brother, "he's a good ball player. The big game is tomorrow, too."

"We'll be there," said Papa, "all of us."

"Sounds like music to me!" Sammy said.

1. Why is "All Except Sammy" a good title for this story?

2. How did Sammy find a way to be in the next family picture?

3. Why did the photographer call the Agabashians "an artistic family"?

4. Do you think Jason was a good friend? Why?

5. Find the clues on page 186 to support Sammy's statement, "That horse could run like the wind."

Sometimes people need to make schedules to help them organize their time. In "All Except Sammy", Sammy could use a schedule to organize his time. Make a schedule for Sammy that shows all the things he does during the week. Use the story to make sure you include all his activities.

Prewrite

Sammy felt left out of his family until he learned to paint. How did learning to paint help Sammy fit in? What else could Sammy have done to fit into his family? What did Sammy have to accept when he chose to go to art class on Saturdays?

Compose

Choose one of the activities below.

1. Sammy let Tug play first base for him when he began to go to art class. Write a paragraph that tells why Sammy was willing to let Tug substitute for him.

2. Besides painting, what else might have helped Sammy fit in with his musical family? Write a paragraph that describes something else Sammy might have done to help him fit in.

Revise

Read your paragraph. Have you written a main idea and supported it with details? Make any changes that are needed.

Biography and Autobiography

A **biography** is the true story of a person's life. It is usually written about the whole life or part of the life of that person. The author of a biography is someone other than the person whose story is being told. The true story of the life of Claude Monet written by someone other than Monet is a biography.

A special kind of biography is called an **autobiography.** When a person writes the true story of his or her own life, the story is called an autobiography. You are the only person who can write your autobiography.

Read the titles and authors of the following books. Which ones are autobiographies?

1. *Anne Frank: The Diary of a Young Girl* by Anne Frank
2. *Annie Oakley and the World of Her Time* by Clifford L. Alderman

3. *Journey into Childhood: The Autobiography of Lois Lenski* by Lois Lenski
4. *Homesick: My Own Story* by Jean Fritz

If you said that *The Diary of a Young Girl, Journey into Childhood,* and *Homesick* are all autobiographies, you are right. *Annie Oakley and the World of Her Time,* however, is not an autobiography because it is the story of Annie Oakley's life told by another person.

Think about the kind of information you might find in a biography and an autobiography. Tell which information from the following list you might find.

1. The time and place the person was born
2. Make-believe stories
3. Who the person's parents were
4. Important events in the person's life

If you said that you might find the time and place the person was born and important events in the person's life, you are right. You might also find out who his or her parents were. You would not find make-believe stories because biographies and autobiographies tell real facts about real people.

The difference between a biography and an autobiography is the person who wrote it.

Tomie dePaola is an award-winning artist and author. What does he write about? Where does he get his ideas?

Meet Tomie dePaola

by Cynthia S. Ciando

The only way to get to Tomie dePaola's house is to go down a winding country road, past a lake and many maple trees. Tomie lives in a farmhouse called Whitebird, tucked into a small New England village.

What was once a barn is now dePaola's studio. On one wall of his studio hangs a pink banner with paper cutouts of some of his characters. Some children in Minnesota gave him this banner. The children shaped the *o* in *Tomie* like a heart because dePaola often uses hearts in his pictures.

Tomie dePaola started to work on children's books by drawing the illustrations for them. He says, "As an artist, it is fairly easy to decide which stories I will do." He sometimes draws the illustrations for other authors' books, but he also writes and illustrates his own books. He says, "Writing my own stories presents a whole different set of problems. The first is that I still find writing difficult. I try not to get set ideas about pictures until after I have written the story. Once the story line is good and strong, then I can let my pictures not only illustrate the story, but add to it."

Some of dePaola's books tell about things that happened when he was little. He mixes the facts with fiction and turns these ideas into stories. He also makes some of his characters seem like his friends or people in his family. The characters in two of his books, *Nana Upstairs and Nana Downstairs* and *Now One Foot, Now the Other,* are very much like his grandparents.

He says that the idea for *The Knight and the Dragon* came from a poster he did for the American Library Association. He remembers that the poster had been hanging on his studio wall for months, when suddenly the idea for the book hit him. "I wish that all ideas were *that* simple," he says. "Children often ask me where I get my ideas. I tell them that I get ideas everywhere. Of course, not every idea is a good one. The boring ones usually go quietly away."

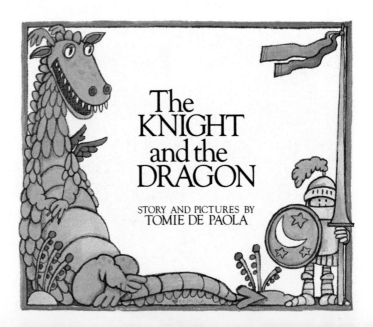

Tomie dePaola has an interesting way of making sure that he doesn't run out of ideas for new books. Before he finishes one book, he usually gets ideas for his next one. "Then I have time to get the old brain and heart going. The important thing is the heart," dePaola says. "It *must* be the best work I can do at the moment."

Tomie dePaola loves children. He says, "I don't think of children as being children. When I find myself in the company of children, I never realize that we're different ages. They're just shorter!" Then that special laugh of his spills out.

When dePaola visited Portland, Oregon, he helped to open a playground. Over 400 children watched as he cut the ribbons holding balloons. Inside the balloons were the children's names, addresses, and telephone numbers. The children hoped they would hear from the people who found the balloons. As the balloons were drifting out of sight, one child whispered, "I hope my balloon lands at Tomie's house."

Tomie dePaola talks with hundreds of children when he is on a trip. He likes to know what they are thinking. He feels it is important for children to meet the authors of the books they like to read. He thinks that "it makes the books come alive for them."

"Books have always been important to me," dePaola says. "My dream is that through writing and drawing pictures, people I've never met will get to know me a little better. I dream that I can somehow touch their lives."

Making a dream like this come true is not always easy—even for a man like Tomie dePaola. "Making a book is one of the hardest things in my life," he says. "Still, I wouldn't have it any other way. Books are my life. Meanwhile, I'll keep working, doing the best I can, and who knows? Maybe that dream will come true."

1. What does Tomie dePaola write about?

2. What are two ways Tomie dePaola gets ideas for his stories?

3. Why does Tomie dePaola write books?

4. Do you think Tomie dePaola will continue writing stories for children? Why?

5. How do you know Tomie dePaola writes his stories before he illustrates them?

A biography is the true story of a person's life. When a person writes his or her own story, it is called an autobiography. Is this selection a biography or an autobiography? How do you know?

Prewrite

You have just studied biography and autobiography. How are a biography and an autobiography the same? How are they different? What information might be the same in both a biography and an autobiography?

Compose

Write a biography of someone you know well, or write your own autobiography. Include the following facts in the biography or autobiography.

1. Who the person is

2. Where the person lives

3. Something about the person's family

4. The person's likes, dislikes, and interests

5. What makes the person special

Revise

Check your work. Have you included all the facts listed above? If not, add sentences to your work to make it complete. Give your biography or autobiography a title.

In this story, how does Bob help Bobby?
How does Bobby help Bob?

Now One Foot, Now the Other

story and pictures by Tomie dePaola

Bobby was named after his best friend, his grandfather Bob. When Bobby was just a baby, his grandfather told everyone, "Bobby will be three years old before he can say Grandpa, so I'm going to have him call me Bob."

"Bob" was the first word Bobby said. Bob was the one who helped Bobby learn to walk.

"Hold on to my hands, Bobby," said his grandfather. "Now one foot, now the other."

When Bobby was older, one of the best things he and Bob did was to play with some old wooden blocks. The blocks had letters on two sides, numbers on two sides, and pictures of animals on the last two sides.

Bob and Bobby would slowly, very slowly, put the blocks one on top of the other, building a tall tower. Sometimes the tower would fall down when only half the blocks were piled up. Sometimes the tower would be almost finished and Bob would say, "Just one more block."

"That's the elephant block," Bobby would say.

They would carefully put the elephant block on the top. Bob would sneeze and the tower would fall down. Bobby would laugh and laugh.

"Elephants always make you sneeze, Bob," Bobby would say.

Then Bob would sit Bobby on his knee and tell him stories. "Bob, tell me the story about how you taught me to walk," Bobby would say.

His grandfather would tell Bobby how he held Bobby's hands and said, "Now one foot, now the other—and before you knew it . . ."

Not long after Bobby's eighth birthday, his grandfather got very sick. Bobby came home from school and his grandfather wasn't there.

"Bob is in the hospital," Dad told Bobby. "He's had what is called a *stroke.*"

"I want to go see him," Bobby said.

"You can't, honey," Mom told him. "Right now Bob's too sick to see anyone. He can't move his arms and legs, and he can't talk. We'll just have to wait and hope Bob gets better."

Bobby didn't know what to do. He didn't want to eat; he had a hard time going to sleep at night. Bob just had to get better.

Months and months and months went by and Bob was still in the hospital. Bobby missed his grandfather.

One day when Bobby came home from school, his father told him that Bob was soon coming home.

"Now, Bobby," Dad said, "Bob is still very sick. He can't move or talk. When he sees your mother and me, he still doesn't recognize us, and the doctor doesn't think he'll get better. Don't be frightened if he doesn't remember you."

Bobby *was* frightened. His grandfather didn't remember him. He just lay in bed. When Dad carried him to the living room, Bob sat in a chair. He didn't talk or even move.

One day, Bob tried to say something to
Bobby, but the sound that came out was awful.
Bobby ran out of the room.

"Bob sounded like a monster!" Bobby cried.

"He can't help it, Bobby," Mom said.

So, Bobby went back to the room where Bob
was sitting. It looked like a tear was coming
down Bob's face.

"I didn't mean to run away, Bob, I was
scared. I'm sorry," Bobby said. "Do you know
who I am?"

Bobby thought he saw Bob blink his eye.

"Mom, Mom," Bobby called. "Bob knows
who I am."

"Oh, Bobby," Mom said. "You're just going
to upset yourself. Your grandfather doesn't
recognize any of us."

Bobby knew better. He ran into the small sewing room, under the front stairs. He took the blocks off the shelf and ran back to where Bob was sitting.

Bob's mouth made a small smile.

Bobby began to build the tower. Halfway . . . almost to the top . . . only one block left.

"Okay, Bob," said Bobby. "Now the elephant block." Bob made a strange noise that sounded like a sneeze. The blocks fell down and Bob smiled and moved his fingers up and down.

Bobby laughed and laughed. Now he knew that Bob would get better.

Bob did get better. Slowly, he began to talk a little. It sounded strange, but he could say "Bobby" just as clear as day. Bob began to move his fingers and then his hands.

When the weather got nice and warm, Dad carried Bob out to a chair set up on the lawn. Bobby sat with him.

"Bobby," Bob said, "story." So, Bobby told Bob some stories.

Then, Bob stood up very slowly.

"You. Me. Walk," said Bob.

Bobby knew exactly what Bob wanted to do. Bobby stood in front of Bob and let Bob lean on his shoulders. "Okay, Bob. Now one foot." Bob moved one foot. "Now the other foot." Bob moved the other.

By the end of the summer, Bob and Bobby could walk to the end of the lawn. Bob could talk better and better each day.

On Bobby's next birthday, Bobby got out the blocks again. Slowly he built up the tower— only one block to go.

"Here, elephant block," Bob said.

Bobby put it on top. Then Bob sneezed!

"Elephants always make you sneeze, Bob," Bobby said. "Now, tell me some stories."

Bob did.

Then Bob said, "Bobby, tell story how you teach Bob to walk."

"Well, Bob, you leaned on my shoulders and then I said, 'Now one foot, now the other,'— and before you knew it . . .''

1. Who was Bob? Who was Bobby?
2. What did Bob do for Bobby? What did Bobby do for Bob?
3. What happened to Bob when Bobby was eight years old?
4. When was Bobby afraid of Bob? Why?
5. How did you know that Bob was unhappy when Bobby ran out of the room?

An *effect* is something that happens, and a *cause* is the reason that something happens. Use information from the story to answer each of the following questions.

1. On page 208, what caused Bobby to think Bob knew who he was?
2. On page 209, what caused Bobby to think that Bob would get better?

Think and Write

Prewrite

Bobby and Bob helped each other because they were best friends. Think about your grandmother and grandfather. What are some special things you might do for them? Think about how you and your best friend help each other.

Compose

Choose one of the activities below.

1. Write a paragraph telling about a special thing you might do for your grandmother, your grandfather, or some other older person you know. Tell how this might help that person.

2. Write a paragraph telling about a special thing you might do for a friend. Tell how this might help your friend.

Revise

Read your paragraph. Did you include all the facts needed to make your paragraph complete? If not, revise your work by adding more facts to your paragraph.

Thinking About "Applause"

In "Applause," you learned that there are different ways of giving applause or praise. Did you also notice that there are many reasons for giving it?

You read about the way deaf people communicate with sign language, and about Hattie, who became the star of the show. You read about Sammy, who learned that playing an instrument was not the only way to fit into his artistic family. You read a short biography about Tomie dePaola. You learned how dePaola shares his thoughts and ideas through the stories he writes and the pictures he draws.

Each character in "Applause" looked for and found special ways to communicate. Some spoke, some used sign language, and others performed on stage. Some characters painted pictures, and others wrote stories. How and why did these characters earn their applause?

As you read other stories, look for the ways that the characters share feelings. How do they give applause or praise?

1. Clapping your hands and saying kind words are ways of giving applause. Which characters in this unit were given applause for good performances?

2. People who help others should be given applause. Which selections had characters who helped other people?

3. If Sammy were to interview Tomie dePaola, what questions might he ask?

4. Which selection in this unit did you like the best? Why?

5. Which character that you read about would you applaud the most? Why?

Read on Your Own

High Sounds, Low Sounds by Franklyn M. Branley. Harper. This book tells how sounds are made. It contains experiments with sound.

Handtalk: An ABC of Finger Spelling and Sign Language by Remy Charlip and Mary Beth Ancona. Scholastic. This book tells about two kinds of sign language: finger spelling and signing.

Cindy, a Hearing Ear Dog by Patricia Curtis. Dutton. This book tells how young dogs are trained to help deaf owners live on their own.

Nana Upstairs and Nana Downstairs by Tomie dePaola. Putnam. A boy enjoys his special friendship with his grandmother and his great-grandmother.

A Pocket for Corduroy by Don Freeman. Viking. This story tells of a little girl who loses her favorite teddy bear when she leaves him at the laundromat.

Grandmama's Joy by Eloise Greenfield. Philomel. A little girl tries to cheer up her grandmother by reminding her of some very important things.

Lisa and Her Soundless World by Edna S. Levine. Human Sciences Press. This book is about an eight-year-old girl who is deaf. It tells how she learns to talk and to understand other people.

Where the River Begins by Thomas Locker. Dutton. Two young boys and their grandfather go on a camping trip to find the beginning of the river that flows by their home.

Chin Chiang and the Dragon's Dance by Ian Wallace. Atheneum. Chin Chiang has had dreams of dancing the dragon's dance. When the day comes, he is afraid he will be too clumsy.

Music, Music for Everyone by Vera B. Williams. Greenwillow. Rosa starts a band with her friends. She earns some money to help out while her grandmother is sick.

The Best Present Is Me by Janet Wolf. Harper. A girl travels to New York City with her family to celebrate her grandmother's birthday. Along the way, she loses the present she has made for her.

Unit 4
Windows

Windows are more than just panes of glass. You can look into a window and see what is happening inside a room. You can look out of a window and see what is happening outside.

Did you ever think that something like your grandmother's old quilt could be a window to the past? How could museums or folktales teach you about the past? Do you think you could learn a lesson from a garden or a treasure chest?

As you read the stories in this unit, you will be looking through many different kinds of windows. Look beyond the words and pictures on each page. Think about how the characters in these stories learn to look at life differently.

Who are the members of the just plain Rosedale Quilting Club? Why was this club formed?

Sam Johnson and the Blue Ribbon Quilt

by Lisa Campbell Ernst

One morning when his wife Sarah was out of town, Sam Johnson found that the awning over the front porch was torn. That night, Sam sat down to mend the tear. He took cloth from Sarah's scrap bag to mend the hole.

At first it was hard work. As the evening passed, Sam began to have fun picking different scraps of cloth. It was morning before he leaned back to look at his night's work.

"How beautiful!" he said. "Just wait until Sarah sees this awning! She'll be mighty proud."

Mrs. Johnson returned later that afternoon. Sam was waiting for her on the porch. "That's very nice, dear," she said, giving the awning a quick look.

"Don't you think it's beautiful, Sarah?" Sam asked. Mrs. Johnson did not answer. Sam went on, "I had *so* much fun doing it, I've decided to join your quilting club!"

"Now, Sam, dear," Mrs. Johnson chuckled. "It's very nice that you enjoyed yourself while I was away, but join my quilting club? Don't be silly."

The next night, Sarah and Sam rode together to the weekly meeting of the Rosedale Women's Quilting Club. When they walked through the door, all the women turned and stared.

Sam cleared his throat. "Good evening," he said. "I've decided to join your club."

After a few seconds, a small chuckle was heard. Then there was another, and another. Soon everyone in the room was laughing— everyone, that is, but Sam.

"Don't be silly," the club president said. "Our most important quilt of the year is coming up. It's the one for the county fair contest. Why don't you go join the men's Checkers Club if you want something to do with your time?"

Sam walked out of the room. The next day he hung posters all around the county, asking the men to meet at his barn.

That evening, Sam spoke to all the men of Rosedale. He told them what had happened, and about the quilt contest at the county fair.

"Are you ready," Sam asked, "to show that we can do more with our hands than plow a field?" "Yes," answered a small group of voices.

"Then we should make a quilt for that contest ourselves!" Everyone clapped and cheered. The Rosedale Men's Quilting Club had just begun. Sam was made president of the club.

The county fair was only a month away. The men met every night in Sam's barn to work on their "Flying Geese" design. The women were also hard at work on their "Sailboats" design. In the week before the fair, each club worked far into the night.

On the day of the contest, each club folded its quilt. Then each quilt was put in the back of a wagon and taken to the fairground. It was a cool, clear morning after a night of heavy rain.

As the two wagons passed through the gates of the fairground, the members of the Rosedale quilting clubs nodded their heads to each other in greeting. Suddenly a huge gust of wind blew up. Both quilts were swept into the air. Each landed in a giant mud puddle!

Neither group could believe what had just happened. "All that work," Sam Johnson groaned. "All those hours and hours. Now look! Ruined!"

Then the women looked at the men's quilt and noticed how beautiful it was. The men saw for the first time that the women's quilt was quite beautiful, too. "You really did a wonderful job," they said to each other. "It's too bad that neither of our groups will win."

"I have an idea!" Sam cried.

All that morning and all that afternoon, the Rosedale Men's Quilting Club and the Rosedale Women's Quilting Club worked together. They carefully cut out the clean parts of each quilt. Then they pieced them together. As the sun set, the last stitches were being made.

Then the judging for the fair began. Elijah Pool's hog won a blue ribbon for being the heaviest hog. Harriet Eyman's apple bread won every baking prize.

As for the quilting contest, the blue ribbon was awarded to the just plain Rosedale Quilting Club.

"What's the name of your unusual design?" Sam Johnson was asked.

He thought for a moment. Then he replied, "Why, 'Flying Sailboats,' of course!"

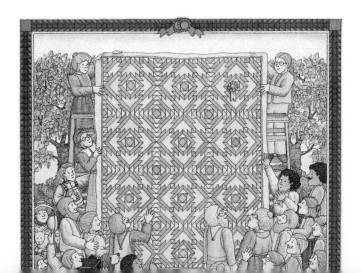

1. What was the "just plain Rosedale Quilting Club?"

2. Why was the club formed?

3. Why was the name "Flying Sailboats" chosen for the quilt?

4. How do you think Sam felt after he went to the Women's Quilting Club meeting?

5. When did you realize that once Sam made up his mind he would not give up?

Writers sometimes give clues to help the reader make predictions about the story. Answer the following questions about the story.

1. On page 221, what clue makes you think that Sam will have trouble joining the women's club?

2. On page 222, what clue makes you think that Sam might start a club for the men?

Prewrite

Sam Johnson found that when people work together, they can usually do a better job than when they work alone. What are some other things that work out better when people work together?

Compose

Choose one of the activities below.

1. Suppose that your family had a large yard with trees and a flower garden. Write a paragraph telling how your family might work together to take care of the yard.

2. Pretend that you are going camping with some friends. Write a paragraph to describe how you and your friends might work together to get ready for the trip.

Revise

Make sure that you have answered each question and included all the details needed to make your paragraph complete.

How is a quilt made? What kinds of quilts do people make?

The Great American Quilt

by Carole Ann Baker

Long ago, it was unusual for old clothes to be thrown away. The parents' old clothes were made smaller to fit their children. Any extra pieces of cloth went into the scrap bag. When the bag was full, it was time to make a patchwork quilt.

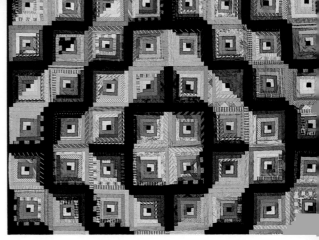

At first, these scraps did not look much like a quilt. They were just pieces of cloth in many colors and sizes. Making all of these scraps look as if they belonged together was one of the jobs of the patchwork quilt maker. The other job was then to stitch the quilt together, using a fancy design.

People who made quilts were like artists without brushes or paint. Tiny bits of cloth and fancy stitches became beautiful designs. The ideas for these quilt designs came from everyday life. One pattern called "Log Cabin" came from the way the logs in a cabin wall looked. Another one, called "Sunshine and Shadow," looked like plowed fields.

Children were taught to quilt as soon as they could hold a needle. Older children sometimes made a quilt to welcome a new baby into a family. These quilts were passed down from family to family.

Making a Quilt

A quilt is made the same way a sandwich is made. Cloth is used for the top and bottom layers, just like bread. Long ago, old cotton, wool, straw, cornhusks, and even old letters were used as stuffing for the quilt.

It took a long time to make a patchwork quilt. Usually, only the top of the quilt was made from the scraps of cloth. Sometimes scraps of cloth were used for both the top and the bottom layers. When it was time for the quilt to be stuffed and stitched together, a quilting bee was often held.

Early in the morning, whole families met in the largest home or town building. The quilters started by stretching the bottom layer of the quilt onto a wooden frame. The quilters sat around the frame to work on the quilt. They sewed three of the edges of the top and bottom layers together. Next the quilt was stuffed. Then the three layers were sewn together with tiny stitches. These stitches were made close together in a design. When all the stitches were done, the last edge was sewn together. Then the quilt was finished.

The quilters worked quickly. They stopped only to eat. Even small children were given an important job. They had to keep the needles threaded for the quilters. That helped the quilters work faster. If more than one person brought a quilt top to the quilting bee, several quilts could be finished in one day.

Friendship Quilts

One kind of quilt is a friendship quilt. Long ago, a friendship quilt was made and given to a person or family who was moving away. It was a sign of friendship from the people who had made the quilt.

The top of a friendship quilt was put together from blocks of cloth. They were all the same size. A group of people would plan the quilt design. Then each person would make a block for the quilt. People's names were sewn onto the quilt block they had made.

Sometimes a saying was sewn on a quilt block. One of the favorite sayings was "When this you see, remember me." Sometimes birds, flowers, or animals made from cloth were stitched onto the quilt block, too. Later all the people would meet to sew the blocks together.

Quilting Today

Many people in America like to save quilts and other things from the past. These old things made by hand help us remember the people who made them. Because quilting is an art form that helps us know about the past, some old quilts are kept in museums.

Today people are still making quilts. They are not just copying old patterns but also are designing new ones. People will probably make quilts for years to come. All that is needed to make a quilt is bits of cloth, needles, thread, and imagination.

1. What quilt patterns were described in this selection?

2. What is needed to make a quilt?

3. Why do some people like to save quilts?

4. Would you rather make or receive a friendship quilt? Why?

5. On page 230, how does the author help you to "see" the layers of a quilt?

The author of "The Great American Quilt" uses both facts and opinions. Read the following sentences from the story. Decide which is a fact and which is an opinion.

1. People who made quilts were like artists without brushes or paint.

2. The quilters started by stretching the quilt's bottom layer onto a wooden frame.

Prewrite

Think about the different kinds of quilts described in the selection. How are quilts like blankets? How are they different? If you were to design a quilt, how would it look?

Compose

Choose one of the activities below.

1. Quilts were made to be used as blankets. Write a paragraph that tells at least two ways in which a quilt is the same as or different from a blanket.

2. Use a piece of paper, a ruler, and crayons to design a quilt pattern. When you have finished your pattern, write a paragraph that tells the name of your pattern and why you designed the quilt the way you did.

Revise

Did you follow the directions in the activity you chose? If not, revise your work.

Follow Directions
Make a Quilted Butterfly

Sam Johnson and the men in Rosedale enjoyed making a quilt for the county fair. People have enjoyed making quilts for hundreds of years. By following directions, you will learn how to make a quilted butterfly.

Here are some things to remember when you follow directions.

1. Read the directions before you begin.
2. Gather your materials. Be sure you have all the things you need before you start your work.
3. Read each step carefully and follow the steps in order.

Things you will need:

an 8½-inch by 11-inch
   piece of paper
a pencil
scissors
two 9-inch by 10-inch
   pieces of fabric
thread

a needle
cotton balls
glue
two buttons
two 5-inch pieces
   of ribbon

1. Fold the piece of paper in half. Starting at the fold, draw half of the butterfly. Cut on the lines you have drawn. Do not cut along the fold. Unfold the butterfly. You now have made a pattern.

2. Lay the pattern on top of the first piece of fabric. Trace the pattern of the butterfly onto the fabric and cut it out. Do the same thing with the second piece of fabric.

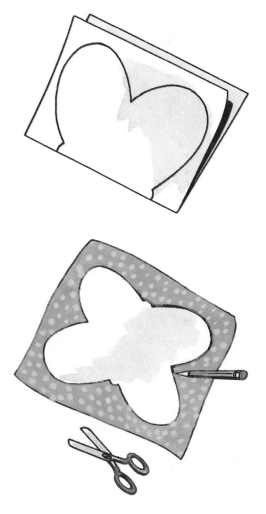

3. Put both pieces of fabric together with the right sides touching.

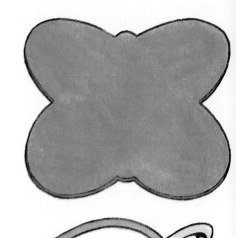

4. Cut a piece of thread about 12 inches long. Thread the needle and then knot the longer piece of thread.

5. Stitch the two pieces of fabric together. Leave openings for the stuffing on each wing. When the pieces have been stitched together, turn the butterfly right-side out.

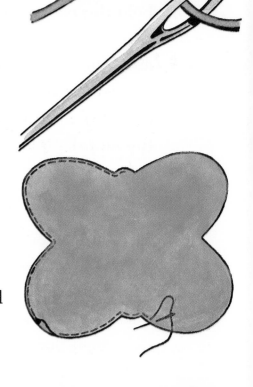

6. Stitch down the middle of the butterfly to make two wings.

7. Stuff each wing with cotton balls. Stitch the open edges closed.

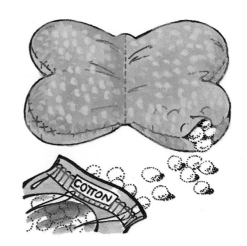

8. Glue two buttons onto the butterfly for its eyes. Glue the two pieces of ribbon onto the butterfly for its feelers.

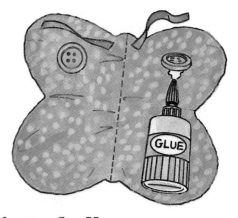

Now you have made a quilted butterfly. You might want to sew a ribbon to your butterfly and hang it in your room. You could even give it to someone as a present.

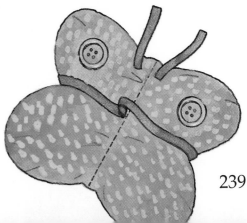

The Miser Who Wanted the Sun

by Jürg Obrist

Once there was a very rich man who was a miser. He lived in a huge house that had many treasures. He slept in a golden bed. He wore golden slippers.

No matter how much he owned, he still wanted more and more treasures. The more he collected, the more he wanted. "He loves gold," people said. "He would even like to own the sun if he could."

"Oh, yes," sighed the miser. "If only I could own the sun! It would make my robes shine like gold." Then he had an idea. What he could have was a robe, as bright and golden as the sun itself.

So he went to the tailor and ordered a golden robe. The tailor shook his head. He had never heard such a strange thing before.

"I'm not worried about the cost," the miser said. "You can choose your payment from my treasure room." The tailor agreed to make the robe.

The tailor cut out the robe from the beautiful golden cloth. The tailor's wife sewed the cloth. The tailor's children, Tim and Lily, sewed on the fine buttons and beautiful gems. They all worked for days and days.

Soon the miser began to worry that the tailor might take too many of his treasures. So, one by one, he hid his treasures in another room. "There's still plenty left for the tailor," he said, and smiled to himself.

The tailor and his children brought the golden robe to the miser. The miser looked at it carefully. "Now you may choose your payment from my treasure room," he told them.

Inside the treasure room there was only one large chest. "The treasures must be in there," the tailor and his children thought. They opened it quickly, but the chest looked empty! Only a tiny golden thimble lay at the bottom.

"Is this our payment?" Tim asked angrily. "Don't worry, this chest will be useful," said Lily. She suddenly had an idea. Tim and Lily lifted the chest onto a cart. Then they pulled it home.

A few days later, Tim and Lily came back to see the miser. "We have heard that it is your greatest wish to own the sun," they said.

"The sun!" the miser sighed. "It's the only thing I still need for my collection of treasures."

"We know how to catch it for you," said Lily. "In return, we want to choose something from your house."

The miser was so excited, he agreed. "You may have whatever your hands can carry."

That evening, the miser watched Tim and Lily from his house, as they had told him to do. They pulled the empty treasure chest up the hill, behind which the sun set each day. At the top of the hill, they opened the lid and waited.

The sun began to set, right into the chest. The miser watched carefully as the last beam of light faded. Then the children quickly shut the lid and brought the chest back to the miser.

"You have certainly earned your payment," the miser said.

"All we want is your golden robe," said the children. They quickly took the robe and carried it home.

The miser had never felt so happy before. Now he was richer than ever! He looked forward to the next day when he could enjoy having the sun all to himself.

The next morning he woke early. He jumped to the window and saw that the sun was rising over the forest, just as it did every day.

"It can't be!" The miser was very angry. He ran to the chest and opened it. The chest was empty! Only the tiny golden thimble lay at the bottom. Now the miser understood that he had to enjoy the sun where it was, like everyone else.

Later that day, the miser went to the tailor and his family. This time, he brought them fair payment for their work. Then they gave him back the golden robe.

As he carried the robe home, it seemed to shine even brighter in the evening sun. "Everyone can share the sun," the miser said, "but no one has a golden robe like mine!"

1. What lesson did the miser learn?

2. Who taught the miser this lesson? How?

3. What did each of the people in the tailor's family do to make the robe?

4. Do you think the miser was happy at the end of the story? Why?

5. How do you know that the miser was not a fair man?

Apply

the

Skills

The writer gave clues in "The Miser Who Wanted the Sun" to help you predict what might happen. Answer the following questions.

1. On page 241, what tells you that there are going to be problems about receiving fair payment for the robe?

2. On page 242, what tells you that the tailor's family may figure out a way to get payment for the golden robe?

Prewrite

Think about how the story would have been different if the miser had owned the sun. What do you think he might have done with it? Do you think he would share the sun with others? Why?

Compose

Write a paragraph that describes what might have happened if the miser had owned the sun. You should include a sentence that tells the main idea of your paragraph. Include at least three descriptive details.

Revise

Read your paragraph. Does it clearly describe the things you are writing about? Add more details to your paragraph if they are needed to make your work complete.

Folktales explain why things are the way they are. Read this folktale to find out how some people explain why spiders live in ceilings.

Why Spider Lives in Ceilings

retold by Joyce Cooper Arkhurst

adapted by Anne Maley

CHARACTERS

Storyteller 1	**Elephant**	**Storyteller 2**
Mother	**Tortoise**	**Storyteller 3**
Girl	**Spider**	
Hare	**Leopard**	

Storyteller 1: Once upon a time the rainy season came to the forest of West Africa, as it must come every year. This time there was more rain than ever before. Nobody had ever seen anything like it. The people in the villages were frightened.

Mother: *(excitedly)* Listen to the rain pounding on our roof! The water pours down with a roar like thunder! *(She opens the door and looks out.)* Water rushes everywhere, and the footpaths look like rivers!

Girl: *(sadly)* Look how the rain beats against the tree branches and tears off their leaves.

Mother: Let us close the door. There is no use looking outside. All we will see is rain, rain, rain!

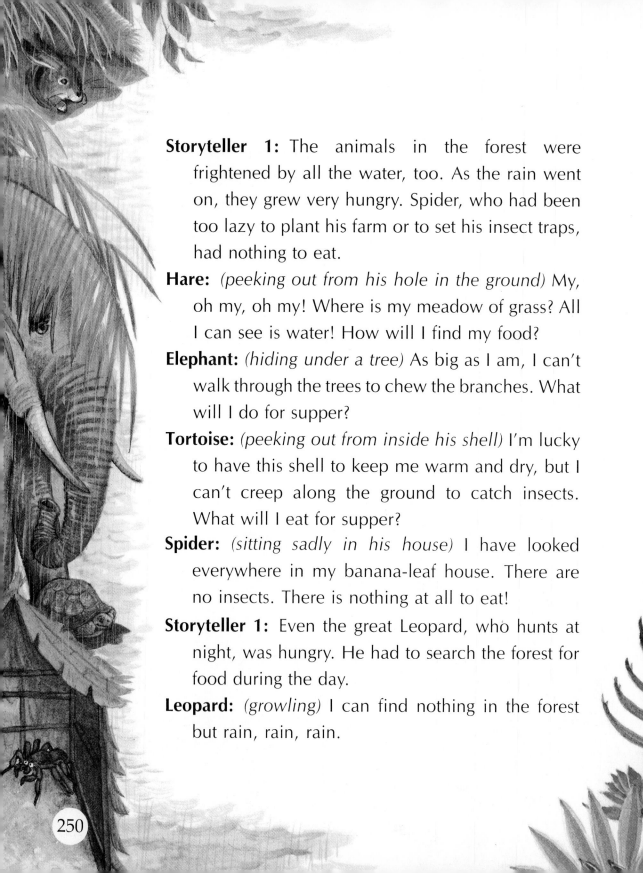

Storyteller 1: The animals in the forest were frightened by all the water, too. As the rain went on, they grew very hungry. Spider, who had been too lazy to plant his farm or to set his insect traps, had nothing to eat.

Hare: *(peeking out from his hole in the ground)* My, oh my, oh my! Where is my meadow of grass? All I can see is water! How will I find my food?

Elephant: *(hiding under a tree)* As big as I am, I can't walk through the trees to chew the branches. What will I do for supper?

Tortoise: *(peeking out from inside his shell)* I'm lucky to have this shell to keep me warm and dry, but I can't creep along the ground to catch insects. What will I eat for supper?

Spider: *(sitting sadly in his house)* I have looked everywhere in my banana-leaf house. There are no insects. There is nothing at all to eat!

Storyteller 1: Even the great Leopard, who hunts at night, was hungry. He had to search the forest for food during the day.

Leopard: *(growling)* I can find nothing in the forest but rain, rain, rain.

Storyteller 2: Then one afternoon, the rain stopped. Spider set out at once to look for something to eat. He went down the wide path that led to the river.

Leopard was hunting, too, with a hungry look in his eye. He walked quietly along the path that led to the river. That is how it happened that Spider and Leopard walked right into each other.

Usually, Leopard loves a fat and juicy supper. But today he thought even a small spider would taste good, so he stopped to chat and tried to look friendly.

Leopard: *(sweetly)* Good afternoon, Mr. Spider. How are you feeling after all this wet weather?

Storyteller 2: Spider was lazy, but he was clever, too. He knew at once that Leopard's voice was much too sweet.

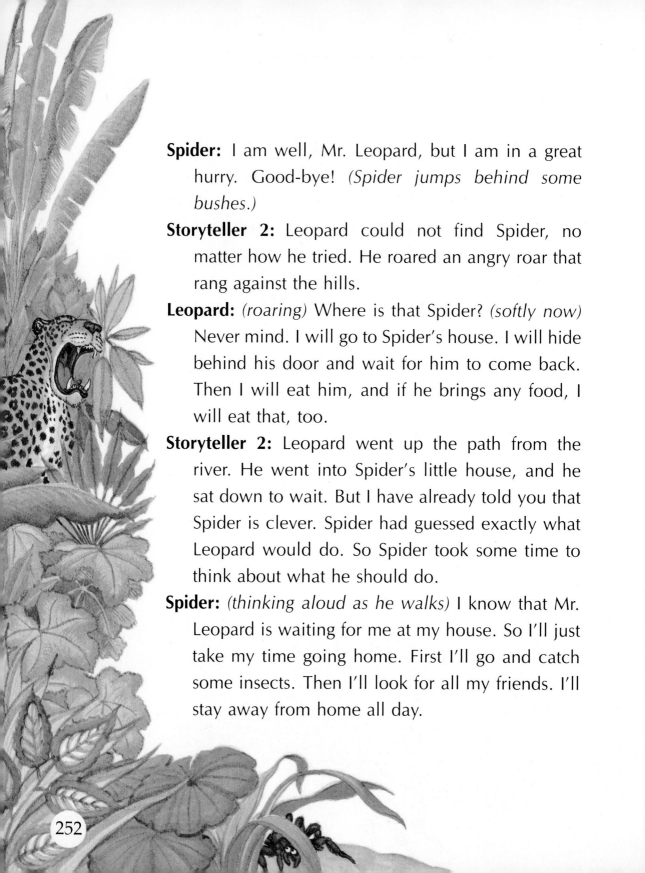

Spider: I am well, Mr. Leopard, but I am in a great hurry. Good-bye! *(Spider jumps behind some bushes.)*

Storyteller 2: Leopard could not find Spider, no matter how he tried. He roared an angry roar that rang against the hills.

Leopard: *(roaring)* Where is that Spider? *(softly now)* Never mind. I will go to Spider's house. I will hide behind his door and wait for him to come back. Then I will eat him, and if he brings any food, I will eat that, too.

Storyteller 2: Leopard went up the path from the river. He went into Spider's little house, and he sat down to wait. But I have already told you that Spider is clever. Spider had guessed exactly what Leopard would do. So Spider took some time to think about what he should do.

Spider: *(thinking aloud as he walks)* I know that Mr. Leopard is waiting for me at my house. So I'll just take my time going home. First I'll go and catch some insects. Then I'll look for all my friends. I'll stay away from home all day.

Storyteller 3: And that is what Spider did. Finally, it began to get dark. The sky filled with clouds, and once again the rain began to fall. At last Spider had to go home. So he went up the path that led past the river and near his little house made of banana leaves.

Spider: *(looking down at the ground)* I don't see Mr. Leopard's tracks. *(He listens hard.)* I don't hear Mr. Leopard's sounds. *(He looks all around.)* But I *know* Mr. Leopard is around here somewhere.

Storyteller 3: Even though Spider saw and heard nothing, he knew the ways of Leopard. So Spider kept walking down the path, humming to himself, just as if he were thinking of nothing. Suddenly he cried out.

Spider: *(shouting)* Hello, my banana-leaf house!

Storyteller 3: Nobody answered. Spider walked a little nearer. Still there was quiet.

Spider: *(loudly)* That's funny. My little house always answers me when I call it. I wonder what is wrong. *(He shouts again, with all his might.)* Hello, my banana-leaf house! How are you?

Storyteller 3: From deep inside the house came a small, high voice.

Leopard: *(speaking in a high little voice)* I am fine, Mr. Spider. Come on in.

Spider: *(laughing)* Ha, ha! Now I know where you are, Mr. Leopard, and you'll never catch me!

Storyteller 3: With that, Spider ran as quick as a flash through the window and up to the highest part of the ceiling. Leopard could not catch him even though he tried and tried. Spider was warm and dry and safe in the ceiling. I suppose that is why he decided to live there, and he is living there still!

1. How does this folktale explain why spiders live in ceilings?

2. Why did Spider and Leopard meet?

3. How did Spider trick Leopard into telling him where he was?

4. Which animal do you think was smarter, Spider or Leopard? Why?

5. How do you know that the water was very high?

A play gives the reader information through stage directions and what the characters say. Use the stage directions and the character's words to answer the following questions.

1. On page 250, how do you know Leopard was angry about not having any food?

2. On page 254, how do you know Spider wants Leopard to overhear him?

Prewrite

The heavy rains in the forest caused problems for both people and animals. For example, the animals were unable to find enough food to eat. What are some other problems the rain could cause? Who could be troubled by the rain?

Compose

Choose one of the activities below.

1. Write a paragraph describing two problems heavy rains may cause. What are the problems? Who had them? How did rain cause them?

2. Write a paragraph describing two ways that the animals might have gotten food during the rain. What kind of food might they have found? Where might they have found it?

Revise

Check your work carefully. Make changes if they are needed.

The Spider Web
by Truda McCoy

The spider spun a silver web
   Above the gate last night.
It was round with little spokes
   And such a pretty sight.

This morning there were drops of dew
   Hung on it, one by one;
They changed to diamonds, rubies red,
   When they were lit with sun.

A spider's nice to have around
   To weave a web so fine.
On which to string the drops of dew
   That catch the bright sunshine.

Predict Outcomes

Look at the picture. Can you tell what might happen? If you can, then you are predicting an outcome. The word **predict** means to tell something you think will happen.

What do you think the woman in the picture might do? Did you say that the woman might climb the ladder and pick the apples? What clues make you think this? The clues are the ripe apples, the ladder, the woman's clothes, and the pail.

You are predicting an outcome when you put clues together and then use these clues to tell what will happen.

Read the paragraph below. Predict what Pam might do. Then tell what clues helped you to think that.

Pam drove to the lake. When she got out of the van, she started to unpack her things. First, she reached for her basket. Then she picked up her bait, hooks, and long pole. She walked toward the lake.

Did you say that Pam was going fishing? What are the clues? Yes, the clues are her bait, hooks, long pole, and the lake.

Sometimes authors do not give you all the clues in a story at once, so your predictions might have to change. As you read more of the story, you get new clues and may have to change your predictions. When you take new clues and put them together with what you already know, and then change your prediction, you are being a good reader.

Now read more about Pam to see if she really does go fishing.

When Pam got to the lake, she dropped her things and quickly opened her basket. She took out her sketch pad and charcoal. She started to sketch the ducks that were swimming in the lake. Before Pam knew it, it was time to go home. Pam never did go fishing.

Did you change your prediction? Why?

As you read, remember to look for clues that help you make predictions about what might happen. Remember, also, to look for new clues and be ready to change your prediction.

In this story, what treasure does a father give to his three sons?

The Buried Treasure

retold by Djemma Bider

Once upon a time, an old man lived high in the mountains. He had a garden, and he worked in it all day long. He loved his garden very much.

His three sons loved the garden, too, but they were lazy fellows. They did not care for hard work. Digging, planting, and carrying water was very hard work.

Still, each of the sons did do something now and then. The oldest went fishing. The middle son went hunting. The youngest son took care of a neighbor's horses. They did not earn much money, because they did not do much work.

The years passed. One day the father became too old to work. He called his sons to him and said, "Dear children, I will tell you a secret. I happen to know there is a treasure buried in my garden. If you keep digging in the earth, sooner or later you will find the treasure."

Not long after, their father died. The sons buried him with great honor.

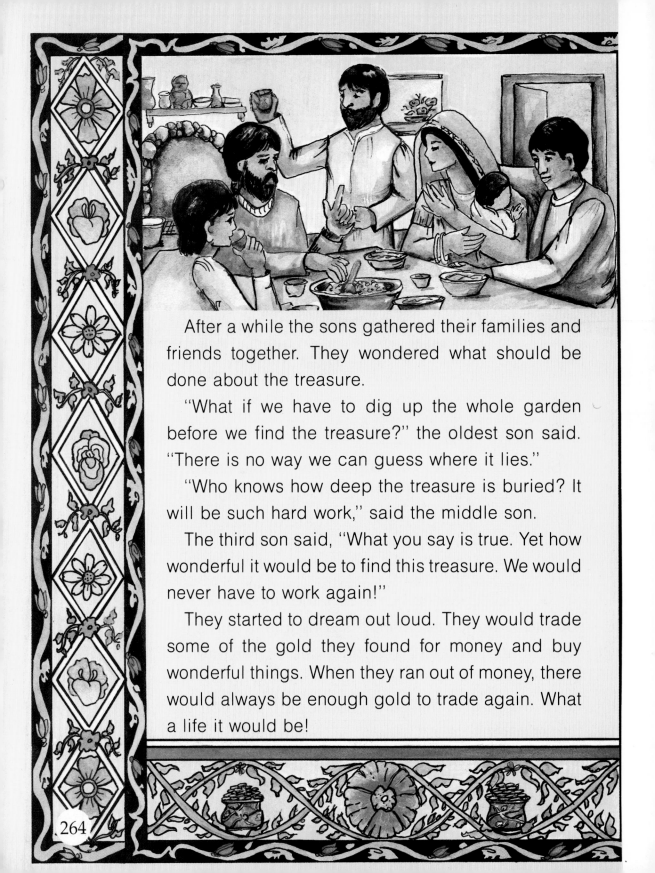

After a while the sons gathered their families and friends together. They wondered what should be done about the treasure.

"What if we have to dig up the whole garden before we find the treasure?" the oldest son said. "There is no way we can guess where it lies."

"Who knows how deep the treasure is buried? It will be such hard work," said the middle son.

The third son said, "What you say is true. Yet how wonderful it would be to find this treasure. We would never have to work again!"

They started to dream out loud. They would trade some of the gold they found for money and buy wonderful things. When they ran out of money, there would always be enough gold to trade again. What a life it would be!

So they got down to work. One morning while they were digging, their favorite uncle passed by. "Good day, my nephews," he said. "How is your work coming along?"

"It's hard going, dear uncle," said the oldest. "Who knows how long it will take us to find the treasure?"

"Indeed, who knows?" answered the uncle. "Since you are digging in the earth anyway, why don't you plant some seeds? Stop by my house. I will give you some."

The uncle gave the brothers many seeds. He gave them all kinds of vegetable seeds. He also gave them seeds for every kind of flower.

That was not all. He gave them young apple, plum, and cherry trees. Someday the brothers would have an orchard.

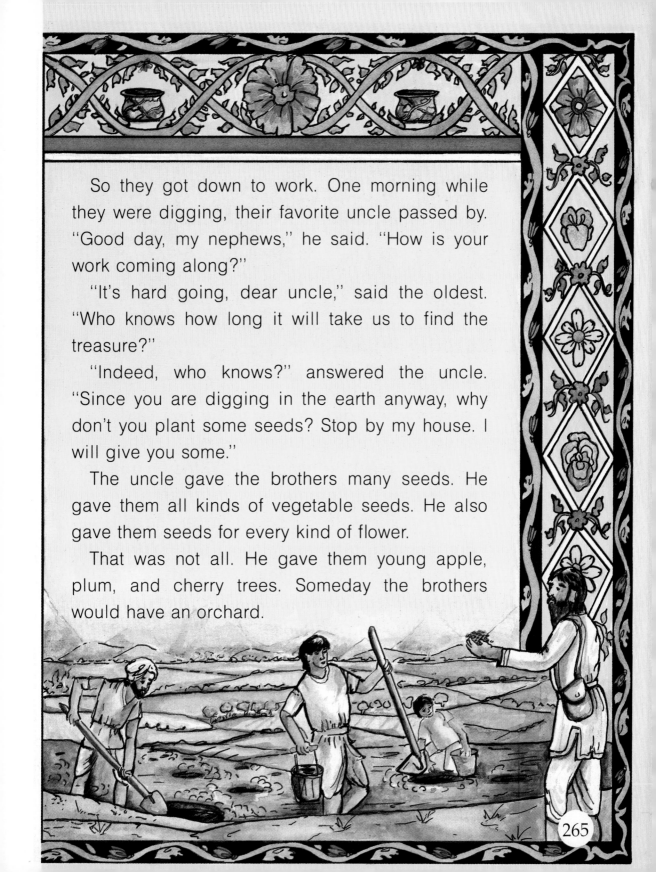

The brothers did as their uncle had said. They planted the seeds as they dug the soil. When they wanted to plant the young trees, they made very deep holes. They watered the soil often.

Day after day they worked under the hot sun. Their muscles grew stronger. As time passed, the brothers began to love their work. They talked less and less about the treasure. Often they forgot the reason they had started digging. After months of hard work, the beautiful flowers, vegetables, and fruit began pushing and peeping through the earth.

At summer's end, the brothers had a fine harvest. They brought their fruit, vegetables, and flowers to the market. Their fruit and vegetables were always the freshest and the ripest. Their flowers were the most beautiful. People from faraway mountain villages came to the market to buy the best fruits, vegetables, and flowers from them.

Year after year, the brothers worked hard. In the fall, they reaped a rich crop. They took flowers and vegetables to the market. They also took apples, plums, and cherries from their orchard. At harvest time, the best parties were always held at the homes of the three brothers.

Finally the three brothers realized how wise their father had been. They understood what their father had meant when he said that sooner or later they would find a treasure in the earth.

1. What did the father mean when he said his sons would find treasure in the garden?

2. What was the treasure?

3. How did the uncle help the brothers find the treasure?

4. What kind of treasure did you think was buried in the garden?

5. When did you know what the treasure was?

A good reader thinks ahead and makes predictions. Answer the following questions about the story.

1. On page 263, what made you think someone would have to dig for the treasure?

2. On page 264, what told you the brothers might look for the treasure?

Prewrite

Think about the treasure the three brothers found. They realized that their father had given them a way to live happily for the rest of their lives. What do we usually think of as a buried treasure?

Compose

Choose one of the activities below.

1. Pretend that someone just gave you a secret map to a buried treasure. Write a paragraph telling what you must do to find the treasure.

2. Pretend that you have found a buried treasure. Write a paragraph that describes the treasure and tells where you found it. It may be a make-believe treasure, or one like the treasure in the story.

Revise

Will someone reading your paragraph understand what you have written? If not, revise your work.

Seeds

by Walter de la Mare

The seeds I sowed—
For weeks unseen—
Have pushed up pygmy
Shoots of green;
So frail you'd think
The tiniest stone
Would never let
A glimpse be shown.
But no, a pebble
Near them lies,
At least a cherry stone
In size,
Which that mere sprout
Has heaved away,
To bask in sun,
And see the day.

Bar Graphs

Amy's teacher asked her to tell how she used her time today. Amy wrote a paragraph telling what she did. Her teacher helped her show the same information in a special drawing called a **bar graph.** Read the paragraph. Then look at the bar graph. Decide which is the easier way to understand how Amy used her time.

There are twenty-four hours in every day. Today I did many things in those twenty-four hours. I spent seven hours in school. I played outside for three hours. I spent three hours eating and one hour doing my homework. I also slept for ten hours.

My Activities

Look at the bar graph. The title tells what is being shown. The labels along the bottom name the things or activities that Amy did. Look at the numerals along the left side. On this bar graph, the numerals show how many hours Amy spent on each activity.

Sometimes bar graphs are drawn so that the bars go across instead of up and down. The numerals on this kind of bar graph are usually placed along the bottom while the things being compared are listed on the left side. This is how Amy's time would look on this kind of bar graph.

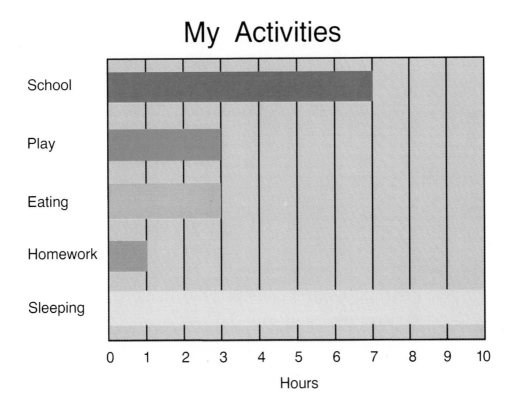

My Activities

Hours

Textbook Application: Bar Graphs in Social Studies

A bar graph is often used in textbooks to help present some information. Read the following paragraph, bar graph, and questions from a social studies textbook. Then use the information on the bar graph to answer the questions.

Learning About Bar Graphs

What was the population (pop′ yə·lā′ shən) of the United States when it won its independence? Population is the number of people who live in a place. Soon after the United States was born, Americans decided to find out the population of their country. In 1790 they made a count, or census, of the population.

Americans learned many things from the first census. They learned that Virginia had the largest population. They learned that Delaware had the smallest population. They also found out which cities had the most people.

Use the bar graph to answer the questions below.

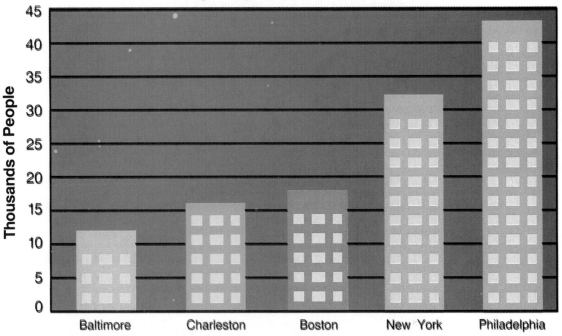

City Population in 1790

Thousands of People (y-axis: 0, 5, 10, 15, 20, 25, 30, 35, 40, 45)

Baltimore · Charleston · Boston · New York · Philadelphia

Practicing Your Skills

1. Which city had the largest population in 1790?
2. Which city had the fewest people?
3. Which cities had fewer than 20,000 people?
4. Which cities had more than 30,000 people?

—Communities: People and Places, Macmillan

Fire Fighting—
Then and Now

by Cheryl Francis

Fire can be helpful to people, but it can also be an enemy. People have had to fight fire from early times. How did they do this?

Long ago in villages and towns, houses could catch fire very easily because they were built of wood and often had straw roofs. Fires often started when sparks from fireplaces landed on a roof. Many fires started during the night. People slept while the fire burned. By the time people woke up, it was often too late to save anything.

To solve the problem of knowing when a fire started, some people began walking through the town at night from nine o'clock until dawn to watch for fires. These people were called "prowlers." Each night, ladders were left on street corners, and buckets of water were left on doorsteps. If a prowler saw a fire, he would shake a wooden rattle. The noise from the rattle would wake the people of the town. Then the prowler would carry the nearest ladder to the fire. By that time, other people would have brought the water buckets and would have been ready to help put out the fire.

Sometimes fires were put out by a "bucket brigade." People made two lines that went to the nearest body of water. They filled buckets with water and handed the filled buckets down one line. The water was thrown on the fire. Then the empty buckets were passed back down the other line to be filled again.

In England during the 1660's, a new way of putting out fires was invented. It was a small wooden box with handles called a hand tub. The hand tub was carried to the fire and then filled with water by the bucket brigade. When the handles on the hand tub were pumped up and down, water shot out onto the fire. This was the first fire-fighting pump. Later, wheels were added to the hand tub so people could pull instead of carry it. Because it could be pulled, the hand tub was made bigger.

Boston, in 1678, was the first American city to order a hand tub from England. Boston was also the first American city to have a paid fire department. It began in 1717 with twenty men. If a fire began in a house, these men would rush to the fire with the hand tub and try to put out the fire.

Other kinds of fire-fighting pumps were made as time went on. Some pumps were small enough to be brought into a home. The closer the pump was to the fire, the easier it was to put out the fire.

Then, steam-engine pumps took the place of hand pumps. The first steam-engine pumps were very heavy. They weighed about 4,000 pounds. Horses were trained to pull the fire wagon with the steam-engine pumps. When the fire bell rang at the firehouse, a good team of trained horses could be ready to go in ten seconds!

Steam-engine pumps did the work of six hand pumps. Only four to six people were needed to run them. In time the steam-engine pumps weighed less and were easier to run. By the year 1900, steam-engine pumps were used in nearly all American cities.

The fire engines that we see today are very different from the early ones. We now have hose trucks with pumps that shoot water onto a fire. There are tankers that bring water to a fire in their water tanks. Another kind of fire engine is called a ladder truck. These trucks need two drivers. One driver steers the front wheels, and the other steers the back wheels.

Fireboats are used to put out fires in lakes, rivers, and oceans. Helicopters throw water on brush fires in forests or on mountains.

Many states have fire-fighting museums.
Some show early fire engines. Visitors to the
New England Fire and History Museum in
Brewster, Massachusetts, can see the old fire
engines, early steam-engine pumps, and hand
tubs. They can also see some of the tools used
by early American fire fighters. These tools
make it easy to imagine what it was like to put
out fires years ago.

1. How did people fight fires before 1900?

2. What are some of the things used to fight fires today?

3. Where can you see some of the tools used by early American fire fighters?

4. If you had lived long ago, would you have liked to have been a prowler? Why?

5. How do you know that steam-engine pumps were better than hand pumps?

An outline of the information in this selection has been started below. On another sheet of paper, copy the outline. Then write three details for each main topic. Label each detail *A*, *B*, or *C*.

Fire Fighting—Then and Now

  I. Early days

 II. Between 1660—1900

III. Today

Prewrite

Think about the ways in which fire fighting has changed over the last three hundred years. One change is that bucket brigades are not often seen today. What other changes have there been?

Compose

Write a paragraph that describes three ways in which fire fighting today is different from fire fighting three hundred years ago. You might describe today's equipment or other inventions that have changed the ways in which fires are fought.

Revise

Did you follow the directions given in the activity you chose? Does your paragraph contain enough details to make your description clear to a reader? If not, revise your work.

What birthday gift did Sumi find to make Ojii Chan's heart sing?

Sumi's Special Happening

by Yoshiko Uchida

Before long, it would be December 5th, and Sumi (sōō'mē) still did not have a birthday gift for Ojii Chan (ō·jē' chən).

Ojii Chan was Gonzaburo Oda (gən·zä' bōō·rō ō'dä). He was the oldest person in the village, and one of Sumi's best friends.

Each year Sumi made him something for his birthday. This year, Mr. Oda was not having an ordinary birthday—he was going to be ninety-nine!

"What shall I give Ojii Chan for this very special birthday?" Sumi wondered.

"Do something to make his heart sing," Mr. Oda's housekeeper told Sumi. The village mayor told her, "If I were ninety-nine, I'm sure I would have all the things I needed. What I would want is a happening."

That night Sumi lay inside her heavy quilts and tried to think of an exciting happening she could bring into Ojii Chan's life. "What can I do?" she wondered. Soon she fell asleep, full of unanswered questions.

The next day was a Sunday. It was the day that Mr. Hattori (hä·tō′rē) always came to visit Father. Mr. Hattori lived in Kasa (kä′sä) Village beyond the wooded hills. Once a month he came on the red bus to spend an afternoon with Father.

Today Mr. Hattori had much to tell. "I am the new one-man fire department of Kasa Village," he said proudly. "I am in charge of the fire truck."

"That is a big job," Father said. "You are able to drive such a truck?"

"Well, it is not exactly a truck," Mr. Hattori explained. "It is an old jeep made to look like a fire truck. We carry some fire-fighting equipment. It is a wonderful sight."

"Does it have a siren?" asked Sumi's brother Taro (tä′rō).

"It does indeed," Mr. Hattori nodded, "and bells—it has many bells."

Sumi wondered what it would be like to ride in such a jeep. In Sugi (sōō′jē) Village no one even owned a car. There was no bus. Anyone could walk from one end of the village to the other in fifteen minutes.

Suddenly, the happening Sumi was searching for popped into her head. Before she could even think of a polite way to ask, she was begging Mr. Hattori for a ride on this wonderful jeep.

"It's not for me," she explained. "It's for Ojii Chan." Quickly she told how she needed a very special happening for Mr. Gonzaburo Oda on his ninety-ninth birthday on December 5th. Sumi was quite sure he had never ridden on a jeep before. Surely he had never in his life ridden on a fire engine jeep.

Mr. Hattori listened to Sumi. He wondered if such a thing would be all right for the one-man fire department of Kasa Village to do. Then he smiled and hit the table with his hand.

"I shall do it," he said. "I will come to take Mr. Oda for a ride. I shall give you *all* a ride such as you have never had in your lives. I will help you give Mr. Oda a day he will never forget!"

"*Banzai!*" (bän′zī) Sumi and her brother Taro shouted together. They could hardly wait for December 5th to come.

Later Sumi told Mr. Mayor of the happening she had decided upon. He shook her hand as though he were giving her an award.

"That is exactly right, exactly right!" he cried. "A happening such as that will surely warm his heart." Then he told Sumi to be sure that their ride ended at the school. "I shall have a happening of my own for Mr. Oda," he said.

When Sumi woke up on December 5th, she saw that it had snowed overnight. Snow was still falling from the sky. How would Mr. Hattori ever get his jeep over the hills with all this snow?

"It's snowing!" Sumi cried, but Mr. Hattori came at the time he had promised. He was wearing a big coat. His cheeks were red from the cold.

Sumi and Taro ran outside. There in front of their house was a red jeep. It was so red, it looked like a big apple. A ladder was tied to its side. Buckets hung from the rear. From a rope strung along its sides hung many bells of every size and shape. First Mr. Hattori gave the rope a tug. The bells rang in the snowy stillness. Sumi clapped her hands.

Next, Mr. Hattori pushed the big horn. It sounded like an angry moose. Then he pulled on a chain that made the siren scream.

Taro could wait no longer. Shouting happily, he climbed onto the fire engine jeep. No one in the world could have pulled him off. Mother and Father heard the noise and hurried outside with the children's coats and hats.

Mother and Father just had time to bow and greet Mr. Hattori. Then, with a great, loud roar, Mr. Hattori started the jeep. He hurried off with Sumi and Taro to Mr. Oda's house.

"Ojii Chan, Ojii Chan!" Sumi shouted as she streaked into his house. "Happy birthday! *Omedeto!* (ō·me·de'tō) Put on your warmest coat and hat. I have a birthday surprise for you!"

"A surprise?" Ojii Chan asked in a thin voice.

"Hurry, Ojii Chan," Sumi begged. Mr. Oda put on his great black cape and his beaver hat. Sumi could hardly wait!

Mr. Oda saw the bright red fire engine jeep at his gate. His mouth fell open into a great "O." He blinked his eyes as though he couldn't believe what he saw.

Mr. Hattori bowed deeply and rang all the bells. Taro squeezed the horn and shouted, "Happy birthday, Ojii Chan!"

"We're taking you for a ride," Sumi said, tugging at Ojii Chan's sleeve. "This is my birthday present. It's a special happening so you won't ever forget your ninety-ninth birthday."

Ojii Chan shook his head. He smiled at the wonderful sight in front of him. He was so pleased he didn't know what to do.

"We shall circle the rice fields of Sugi Village three times. Then we shall go to the village school," Mr. Hattori said. Carefully he helped Mr. Oda into the jeep. Then he shouted, "Now, let us go!" Away they roared down the road like a noisy red bull.

The one-man fire department of Kasa Village made the siren scream and the bells ring. They rumbled past snow-covered fields. By the second time they went around the village, people came outside. They stood in front of their houses to see what all the noise was about.

"It's Ojii Chan's birthday!" Sumi and Taro shouted together at all the wondering faces. When they heard, the villagers laughed and waved and shouted, *"Banzai! Banzai!"*

Many of the village children followed the noisy red jeep. At last it reached the school. The yard was already filled with the laughing, shouting children, and many of their parents.

Mr. Mayor hurried out to greet them. *"Omedeto!* Congratulations!" he said, smiling and bowing to Mr. Oda. "Please step inside and warm yourself."

They all went inside. Sumi saw that the mayor had made a fine happening of his own. His wife had come with him. She had set up a table covered with a red and white cloth.

On the table were plates heaped with food. The news of Mr. Oda's birthday had spread quickly. Now other villagers came, bringing tins of crackers, fruit, and anything they could find in their homes. Sumi's mother and father came carrying their gifts.

"It's a big party!" Sumi said happily.

"It's the best thing that's happened all year," Taro added.

Mr. Oda was so happy he sniffled into his big white handkerchief. Mr. Mayor stood up and told Mr. Oda how happy he was that they had all been able to celebrate his ninety-ninth birthday with him. He told how Sumi's happening had given him the idea for this party.

Everyone agreed that it was the nicest happening to have come along in a long, long time. They came to pat Sumi on the head. They told her how pleased they were that she'd had such a fine idea. Ojii Chan himself told her that he'd never had a finer birthday in all his life.

When it was time to go home, Mr. Oda thanked everyone who had come. Then he returned happily to the fire engine jeep for the ride home.

"Blow your horn, Mr. Fire Department!" Mr. Oda called out. "Blow your siren! This time *I* am going to ring your bells." He reached for the rope strung with the bells and rang them just as hard as he could.

"Ojii Chan, *banzai!*" everyone shouted. In a blaze of wonderful noise they roared back to Mr. Oda's house.

They made such a loud noise that Ojii Chan's housekeeper came rushing to the gate. "Are you all right?" she asked him.

"Of course I'm all right," Mr. Oda said. "I have just had more fun today than I have had in a very long time."

The old housekeeper nodded. "I can tell," she said. "It is there for all to see on your face." Then she smiled at Sumi. "The heart is singing, little one," she said. "You gave him the best gift of all."

1. Why did Sumi want to give Ojii Chan a special birthday gift?

2. What was Sumi's birthday gift to Ojii Chan?

3. How did Mr. Hattori's visit help Sumi?

4. How do you think Sumi felt at the end of the story? Why?

5. When did you know that Ojii Chan liked his birthday gifts?

Apply the Skills

Authors give clues in their stories to help the reader draw conclusions. Read the following conclusions. Then find details in the story to support each conclusion.

1. Sumi cares very much for Ojii Chan.

2. Ojii Chan is well-liked by the whole town.

3. Mr. Hattori is a kind man.

Thinking About "Windows"

In this unit, you learned that there are different kinds of windows. Some windows can show you what things were like long ago. Other windows can help people see themselves more clearly.

You read old tales about a miser, a clever spider, and three lazy brothers. These old stories have been told over and over again by many people. What lessons did the characters in these stories learn? What lessons did you learn?

You read how museums can show what life was like a long time ago. What story might an old fire engine or an old quilt tell?

Sumi looked into her own heart and tried to predict what would make Ojii Chan happy. Were her predictions correct?

As you read other stories, look for those that are windows to the past. Look also for those stories that have different kinds of windows.

1. The word *window* doesn't mean just the kind of windows you find in a house. Which stories in this unit are "windows to the past" because they tell about things that happened long ago?

2. New ways of looking at something can be "windows to learning." Which characters that you read about learned something new?

3. How are the miser, Tim and Lily, Spider, and Leopard alike? How are they different? Why?

4. Both Sam Johnson and Sumi had problems. What were these problems, and how were they solved?

5. If you could learn more about one of the characters in this unit, which character would you choose? Why?

Read on Your Own

The Adventures of Spider by Joyce Cooper
  Arkhurst. Little, Brown. "Why Spider Lives in
  Ceilings" was taken from one chapter in this
  book of West African folktales. Read the rest
  to find out more about Spider.

Fireman Jim by Roger Bester. Crown. This book
  tells about a day in the life of a fire fighter. He
  takes part in a fire drill and fights a real fire.

A New True Book: Fire Fighters by Ray Broekel.
  Childrens Press. This book tells about the
  work, tools, and special clothing of fire
  fighters. It also tells about different kinds of
  fire trucks.

Harlequin and the Gift of Many Colors by Remy
  Charlip and Burton Supree. Four Winds.
  Harlequin's friends give him a special gift so
  that he can make his own costume to wear to
  Carnival.

Be Nice to Spiders by Margaret Bloy Graham. Harper. This is a story about a spider who went to live at the zoo. After she arrives, the zoo becomes a happier place.

The Spider by Margaret Lane. Dial. Different kinds of spiders and their habits are described in this book. It also tells why spiders are important.

A New True Book: Spiders by Illa Podendorf. Childrens Press. This book tells where spiders live, what they eat, and how they move. It also tells how spiders help and harm people.

The Birthday Visitor by Yoshiko Uchida. Scribner's. Emi is surprised when a visitor from Japan helps make her birthday special. The visitor is not at all what Emi expects.

The Seeing Stick by Jane Yolen. Harper. This is a Chinese tale about how an old man teaches the emperor's blind daughter to see.

Glossary

The glossary is a special dictionary for this book. The glossary tells you how to spell a word, how to pronounce it, and what the word means. Often the word is used in a sentence. Different forms of the word may follow the sentence. If one of the different forms is used in the book, then that form may be used in the sentence.

A blue box ■ at the end of the entry tells you that an illustration is given for that word.

The following abbreviations are used throughout the glossary: *n.,* noun; *v.,* verb; *adj.,* adjective; *adv.,* adverb; *interj.,* interjection; *prep.,* preposition; *conj.,* conjunction; *pl.,* plural; *sing.,* singular.

An accent mark (') is used to show which syllable receives the most stress. For example, in the word *granite* [gran' it], the first syllable receives the most stress. Sometimes in words of three or more syllables, there is also a lighter mark to show that a syllable receives a lighter stress. For example, in the word *helicopter* [hel' ə ·kop' tər], the first syllable has the most stress, and the third syllable has lighter stress.

The symbols used to show how each word is pronounced are explained in the "Pronunciation Key" on the next page.

Pronunciation Key*

a	add, map	m	move, seem	u	up, done
ā	ace, rate	n	nice, tin	û(r)	burn, term
â(r)	care, air	ng	ring, song	yōo	fuse, few
ä	palm, father	o	odd, hot	v	vain, eve
b	bat, rub	ō	open, so	w	win, away
ch	check, catch	ô	order, jaw	y	yet, yearn
d	dog, rod	oi	oil, boy	z	zest, muse
e	end, pet	ou	pout, now	zh	vision, pleasure
ē	equal, tree	o͝o	took, full	ə	the schwa,
f	fit, half	o͞o	pool, food		an unstressed
g	go, log	p	pit, stop		vowel representing
h	hope, hate	r	run, poor		the sound spelled
i	it, give	s	see, pass		a in *above*
ī	ice, write	sh	sure, rush		e in *sicken*
j	joy, ledge	t	talk, sit		i in *possible*
k	cool, take	th	thin, both		o in *melon*
l	look, rule	t̶h̶	this, bathe		u in *circus*

*The Pronunciation Key and the short form of the key that appears on the following right-hand pages are reprinted from the *HBJ School Dictionary,* copyright © 1985 by Harcourt Brace Jovanovich, Inc.

A

aboard [ə·bôrd′] *adv.* **1** On, in, or into a train, plane, or balloon. **2** *prep.* On, in, or into: They gave us something to eat *aboard* the plane.

activity [ak·tiv′ə·tē] *n.* A thing being done: We thought of two *activities* for this morning. *pl.* **activities**

actor [ak′tər] *n.* A person who plays parts in plays and moving pictures. *pl.* **actors**

aeronaut [âr′ə·nôt] *n.* A person who flies a balloon or airplane. ■

agency [ā′jən·sē] *n.* A place or group where business is done for others: After the robbery they went to a detective *agency* for help.

agree [ə′grē′] *v.* **1** To believe the same thing as another person: I *agreed* with what he said. **2** To say yes to: Have you *agreed* to go to the show? **agreed**

alarm [ə·lärm′] **1** *v.* To upset: The loud noise *alarmed* the baby. **alarmed 2** *n.* A bell used as a warning: Did you hear the *alarm* ring?

among [ə·mung′] *prep.* In a group of: His poems were *among* the best in the book.

ancestor [an′ses·tər] *n.* A person in one's family who lived earlier: My father's *ancestors* were from China. *pl.* **ancestors**

angry [ang′grē′] *adj.* Feeling anger. He jumped up *angrily*. *adv.* **angrily**

arch [ärch] *n.* Rounded piece of material over an open place: There was a stone *arch* over the gate. ■

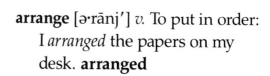

arrange [ə·rānj′] *v.* To put in order: I *arranged* the papers on my desk. **arranged**

artistic [är·tis′tik] *adj.* Showing skill in music or art: My *artistic* sister can draw beautiful pictures and can also play the piano well.

attach [ə·tach′] *v.* To connect: Joe *attached* the string to the kite. **attached**

attention [ə·ten′shən] *n.* The power to keep one's mind on something: The clown danced to get her *attention.*

audience [ô′dē·əns] *n.* A group of people who come to listen to or watch something, as a concert or play: The *audience* liked the band music.

author [ô′thər] *n.* A person who has written a book or story. *pl.* **authors**

award [ə·wôrd′] *n.* A prize: Her painting got an *award.*

awning [ô′ning] *n.* A cover, often made of canvas, used over a window or door for protection from sun or rain. ■

B
---

backstage [bak′stāj′] *adv.* In the part of a theater behind and to the sides of the stage: The class went *backstage* after the play.

badger [baj′ər] *n.* A small animal with short legs, a wide back, and thick fur. ■

bait [bāt] *n.* Food put on a hook or in a trap to catch fish or animals: We use worms as *bait* when we go fishing.

beam [bēm] *n.* A ray of light: The first *beam* of sun shining through my window woke me up.

a	add	o	odd	oi	oil
ā	ace	ō	open	ou	pout
â	care	ô	order	ng	ring
ä	palm	o͝o	took	th	thin
e	end	o͞o	pool	th	this
ē	equal	u	up	zh	vision
i	it	û	burn		
ī	ice	yo͞o	fuse		

ə = { a in *above* e in *sicken* i in *possible*
     { o in *melon* u in *circus*

305

bee [bē] *n.* A gathering of people for work or a contest: Our team won the spelling *bee* this week.

beyond [bi·yond′] *prep.* On the far side of: The animals lived in the forest *beyond* the mountain.

bicycle [bī′sik·əl] *n.* A machine with two large wheels and pedals, on which a person rides. *pl.* **bicycles**

bore [bôr] *v.* To make tired by being uninteresting or dull: The people were *bored* by the long play. **bored, boring**

bought [bôt] *v.* To have paid money for: She *bought* a kite.

brake [brāk] *n.* Things that slow or stop turning wheels: The car will stop when you use the *brakes. pl.* **brakes**

bravo [brä′vō] *interj.* What people call out when someone has done a good job: The people shouted *"Bravo!"* when she won the race.

breakdown [brāk′doun′] *n.* The failing of a machine: There was a computer *breakdown* at the bank.

breathe [brēth] *v.* To take air into the body and then let it out: He had to *breathe* hard after the race.

brigade [bri·gād′] *n.* A group of people who work together to get something done: The bucket *brigade* put out the fire.

burro [bûr′ō] *n.* An animal like a small donkey, used for riding or carrying things. ■

bury [ber′ē] *v.* To put into the ground: The dog looked for the bone it had *buried.* **buried**

C

---

canvas [kan′vəs] *n.* A heavy cloth on which people paint pictures: The artist filled the *canvas* with bright colors.

census [sen′səs] *n.* A counting of people: After the *census* was taken, we knew how many people lived in our town.

charcoal [chär′kōl′] *n.* A black material made by burning wood, which may be used for drawing or for heat.

chat [chat] *v.* To talk in a friendly way: The two old friends stopped to *chat* in the park.

chuckle [chuk′əl] **1** *n.* A soft laugh: Becky heard a *chuckle* coming from the porch. **2** *v.* To laugh softly: Sammy *chuckled* when he heard the joke.
chuckled

clang [klang] *v.* To make a loud ringing sound: We heard the bell *clang*.

cloth [klôth] *n.* **1** A material such as cotton or wool: We found a piece of pretty blue *cloth* for my new dress. **2** A piece of material used in a special way: Mother put the bright red *cloth* on the table.

collection [kə·lek′shən] *n.* The things brought together for study or for saving: He showed me his stamp *collection*.

company [kum′pə·nē] *n.* A group of people working together as a business: The moving *company* has many vans.

concert [kon′sûrt] *n.* A musical performance: He played the drums at the spring *concert*.

congratulation [kən·grach′ə·lā′shən] *n.* The act of expressing good wishes because something good has happened to someone else: We gave him our *congratulations* when he won the contest. *pl.* **congratulations**

contest [kon′test] *n.* A game or race in which prizes are often given: Sam won first prize in the singing *contest*.

cornhusk [kôrn′husk′] *n.* The heavy leaf around an ear of corn: A doll can be made out of *cornhusks*. *pl.* **cornhusks** ■

a	add	o	odd	oi	oil
ā	ace	ō	open	ou	pout
â	care	ô	order	ng	ring
ä	palm	o͝o	took	th	thin
e	end	o͞o	pool	th	this
ē	equal	u	up	zh	vision
i	it	û	burn		
ī	ice	yo͞o	fuse		

ə = { a in *above* e in *sicken* i in *possible*
       o in *melon* u in *circus* }

county [koun′tē] *n.* One of the places into which a state is divided: We live in the largest *county* in the state.

create [krē·āt′] *v.* To make for the first time: He will *create* a picture to win the prize.

crop [krop] *n.* Anything grown on a farm: We have grown many different *crops* on our farm. *pl.* **crops**

cross [krôs] *adj.* Angry: He spoke *crossly* to me. *adv.* **crossly**

crowd [kroud] *n.* A large group of people gathered together. *pl.* **crowds**

curtain [kûr′tən] *n.* A piece of cloth hung in front of a stage or window: He pulled the *curtains* open to let the sun in. *pl.* **curtains** ■

D

dam [dam] *n.* Walls built to hold back water: Sometimes lakes form when *dams* are built on a stream. *pl.* **dams** ■

dawn [dôn] *n.* The first light of day: At camp, we got up at *dawn.*

dead [ded] *adj.* Without life: The wind blew the *dead* leaves into the yard.

delicious [di·lish′əs] *adj.* Having a very good taste: Jason made *delicious* pancakes for breakfast.

design [di·zīn′] **1** *n.* A plan or sketch to be used as a pattern for making something: She wanted a flower *design* on her walls. **2** *v.* To make plans for making something: He will *design* new scenery for the play.

diary [dī'(ə·)rē] *n.* A person's record of what happens every day: He forgot to write in his *diary* this week.

difficult [dif'ə·kult] *adj.* Hard to do: He found that writing a song was *difficult.*

disappoint [dis'ə·point'] *v.* To make unhappy because something did or did not happen: I was *disappointed* when I lost the race.
disappointed

drift [drift] *v.* To move or float on air or water: The balloon *drifted* high over the trees.
drifted, drifting

dusty [dus'tē] *adj.* Full of or covered with dust: The table was *dusty.*

E

---

easel [ē'zəl] *n.* A folding frame with three legs, often used for holding an artist's painting. ■

encore [än(g)'kôr] *interj.* A call made by people to perform again: "*Encore, encore!*" the people shouted after the play.

energy [en'ər·jē] *n.* **1** Lively force or activity: By four o'clock, I had very little *energy* left. **2** Heat or electric power: In our house, we try to use *energy* wisely.

exist [ig·zist'] *v.* To be: Dragons do not *exist* in the real world.

F

---

fabric [fab'rik] *n.* A material, such as cloth or silk: His shirt was made of a silk *fabric.*

face [fās] *v.* To turn in the direction of: Our old house *faced* a lake. **faced**

a	add	o	odd	oi	oil
ā	ace	ō	open	ou	pout
â	care	ô	order	ng	ring
ä	palm	ŏŏ	took	th	thin
e	end	ōō	pool	th	this
ē	equal	u	up	zh	vision
i	it	û	burn		
ī	ice	yōō	fuse		

ə = { a in *above* e in *sicken* i in *possible*
       o in *melon* u in *circus* }

fan [fan] *n.* A person who gets excited about a sport: The baseball *fans* shouted loudly at the game. *pl.* **fans**

fear [fir] *n.* A feeling that danger is near: His *fear* of the dark went away as he grew older.

fierce [firs] *adj.* Very strong, frightening: A *fierce* storm came up suddenly.

figure [fig'yər] *v.* To think about and solve: She will *figure* out how we can get to the circus.

flood [flud] *n.* A great flow of water: The rain brought on a *flood.*

fond [fond] *adj.* Having a liking for or love of: My father is *fond* of our new cat.

formation [for·mā'shən] *n.* Something made into a certain shape: We saw two rock *formations* that looked like bridges in the desert. *pl.* **formations**

fortune [fôr'chən] *n.* A lot of money: He made a *fortune* when he sold his business.

fright [frīt] *n.* Sudden fear: I sat up in *fright* when I heard the scream. **frightened**

fuddy-duddy [fud'ē·dud'ē] *n.* Someone who has no new ideas: They called him a *fuddy-duddy* because he would not read any new books.

fuel [fyo͞o'əl] *n.* Something that makes energy when burned for heat: Wood was the only *fuel* they had at the camp.

G

gem [jem] *n.* A cut and polished stone. The green *gem* was put into a ring.

gondola [gon'də·lə] *n.* A basket that hangs from a hot-air balloon. ■

granite [gran'it] *n.* A hard rock, often used as a building material: The building was made from blocks of *granite.*

graph [graf] *n.* A diagram used to show information: My mother keeps a *graph* to show how tall I am. *pl.* **graphs**

grief [grēf] *n.* Deep sadness: He felt *grief* when he lost his dog.

grumble [grum'bəl] *v.* To make unhappy sounds: She *grumbled* when the rain began. **grumbled**

gust [gust] *n.* A sudden rush of air: The *gust* of wind took the kite high up into the air.

H

halfway [haf'wā'] *adj.* In the middle, between two points: Your house is *halfway* between my house and school.

handkerchief [hang'kər·chif] *n.* A small piece of cloth used to wipe the face and nose: My uncle always carries a white *handkerchief* in his pocket.

handlebar [han'dəl·bär'] *n.* A bar used to steer, as on a bicycle. *pl.* **handlebars**

hare [hâr] *n.* An animal like a rabbit, able to run very fast.

harvest [här'vist] *n.* The gathering and bringing in of a crop: The farmer was glad he had a good *harvest* this year.

haunted [hôn'tid] *adj.* Visited by ghosts: My brother said the old house on the corner was *haunted*.

heap [hēp] *v.* To pile up: I *heaped* the leaves into a big pile and jumped into it. **heaped**

hedge [hej] *n.* A fence formed by bushes planted close together: The horse jumped over the *hedge* and ran away. ■

a	add	o	odd	oi	oil
ā	ace	ō	open	ou	pout
â	care	ô	order	ng	ring
ä	palm	ŏŏ	took	th	thin
e	end	ōō	pool	ŧħ	this
ē	equal	u	up	zh	vision
i	it	û	burn		
ī	ice	yōō	fuse		

ə = { a in *above* e in *sicken* i in *possible*
     o in *melon* u in *circus* }

helicopter [hel′ə·kop′tər] *n.* An aircraft lifted and moved by an engine on top, able to move in any direction: The *helicopter* flew just above the water.

helmet [hel′mit] *n.* A hard covering worn to protect the head: She wears a *helmet* when she goes skating. *pl.* **helmets**

history [his′tə·rē] *n.* A record of past times: There are many things in the museum that tell about the *history* of our town.

honor [on′ər] *n.* Respect: The people gave great *honor* to their hero.

horn [hôrn] *n.* An instrument that sounds a warning: The clown pushed the *horn* on the car.

I

---

illustrate [il′ə·strāt] *v.* To draw pictures for books: Jamie is going to *illustrate* a book about animals. **illustrates**

illustration [il′ə·strā′shən] *n.* A picture in a book: The *illustration* was made in bright colors. *pl.* **illustrations**

imagination [i·maj′ə·nā′shən] *n.* The power to picture something in the mind: The girl used her *imagination* to tell stories to the children.

imagine [i·maj′in] *v.* To form an idea of: I can *imagine* what a dragon looks like.

independence [in′di·pen′dəns] *n.* Freedom: Many people like to have a feeling of *independence*.

insect [in′sekt] *n.* A small animal with six legs and usually two pairs of wings: Flies are *insects. pl.* **insects** ■

invention [in·ven′shən] *n.* Something made for the first time: We saw several *inventions* in the museum. *pl.* **inventions**

inventor [in·ven′tər] *n.* A person who makes something no one has made before: The *inventor* made a new kind of electric light. *pl.* **inventors**

isle [īl] *n.* A small piece of land surrounded by water: The little *isle* in the sea was covered with unusual plants. *pl.* **isles**

J

jade [jād] *n.* A hard stone, usually green, used as a gem: He wanted a *jade* ring.

judge [juj] *n.* A person who decides the winner of a race or game: The *judges* gave the prize to the fastest runner. *pl.* **judges**

juggler [jug′lər] *n.* One who keeps a number of things moving in the air by tossing and catching them: The *juggler* in the circus had a great act.

K

knelt [nelt] *v.* Rested on one's knees: Peggy *knelt* down to look at her garden.

knot [not] *n.* A fastening made by tying ropes together: He made a *knot* in the rope to hold the dog.

L

ladder [lad′ər] *n.* Steps that can be folded and carried from place to place: The painter used a *ladder* to reach the top of the house. *pl.* **ladders** ■

lap [lap] *n.* One time around a race track: The runner ran two *laps* to warm up before the race. *pl.* **laps**

layer [lā′ər] *n.* One covering or thickness: We used only one *layer* of paint on the table. *pl.* **layers**

lesson [les′(ə)n] *n.* Something to be learned: I start my music *lessons* today. *pl.* **lessons**

a	add	o	odd	oi	oil
ā	ace	ō	open	ou	pout
â	care	ô	order	ng	ring
ä	palm	o͝o	took	th	thin
e	end	o͞o	pool	th	this
ē	equal	u	up	zh	vision
i	it	û	burn		
ī	ice	yo͞o	fuse		

ə = { a in *above* e in *sicken* i in *possible*
   o in *melon* u in *circus* }

lily [lil'ē] *n.* A kind of flower:
White *lilies* grew in the yard
near the house. *pl.* **lilies**

limestone [līm'stōn'] *n.* A kind of
rock: They found pieces of
limestone on the hill next to the
beach.

lip-read [lip'rēd] *v.* To find out
what someone is saying by
looking at the lips of the
person speaking, done
especially by the deaf. *n.*
lipreading

lucky [luk'ē] *adj.* Having good
luck: I sometimes feel *lucky*
when I enter a race.

M

mammoth [mam'əth] *n.* A large
animal like an elephant, with
hairy skin, that lived long ago:
I saw a picture of a *mammoth*
in the museum. ■

mark [märk] *n.* A spot or place:
The racer stood on his *mark*.

market [mär'kit] *n.* A place where
many kinds of things are sold:
We sold our flowers at the
town *market*.

material [mə·tir'ē·əl] *n.* That from
which something is made: We
have all the *material* we need
to make the boat. *pl.* **materials**

mayor [mā'ər] *n.* The person who
leads a city or town: The *mayor*
was chosen by the people.

meanwhile [mēn'(h)wīl'] *adv.* In
the time between: I want to go
on vacation next Tuesday, but
meanwhile, I will keep going to
work.

member [mem'bər] *n.* A person
who belongs to a group, as a
family or club: We wanted to
be *members* of the singing
group. *pl.* **members**

mesa [mā'sə] *n.* A hill with a flat
top and steep sides: They
camped on top of the *mesa*.

message [mes'ij] *n.* News or other
communication sent to
another person: Jane sent me
an important *message* in the
mail.

mighty [mī′tē] *adj.* Very strong: A *mighty* wind blew down the tree.

million [mil′yən] *n.* A thousand thousands, written as 1,000,000. *pl.* **millions**

mirror [mir′ər] *n.* A glass in which people can see themselves: I used a *mirror* to see how my clothes looked.

miser [mī′zər] *n.* A person who saves money because he or she loves it: The *miser* loved to count his money.

muscle [mus′əl] *n.* A part of the body that makes the body move: My *muscles* grew stronger when I exercised. *pl.* **muscles**

musician [myo͞o·zish′ən] *n.* A person who is skilled in music: My mother is a fine *musician*. *pl.* **musicians**

N

natural [nach′ər·əl] *adj.* Made in or on the earth, instead of by people: Bear Lake is a *natural* body of water.

nervous [nûr′vəs] *adj.* Feeling upset or very excited: Many people are *nervous* before they take a test.

nylon [nī′lon] *n.* A strong material used to make clothes, rope, and other things: The dress felt like silk, but it was made of *nylon*.

O

orchard [ôr′chərd] *n.* A large group of trees grown for their fruit: The farmer tended his apple *orchard* with great care. ■

a	add	o	odd	oi	oil
ā	ace	ō	open	ou	pout
â	care	ô	order	ng	ring
ä	palm	o͝o	took	th	thin
e	end	o͞o	pool	th	this
ē	equal	u	up	zh	vision
i	it	û	burn		
ī	ice	yo͞o	fuse		

ə = { a in *above* e in *sicken* i in *possible*
     o in *melon* u in *circus* }

ordinary [or′də·ner′ē] *adj.* Not special: It was an *ordinary* van like all the others in the park.

oversized [o′vər·sīzd′] *adj.* Larger than most: My puppy has *oversized* feet.

***

P

pale [pāl] *adj.* A whitish color: She turned *pale* when she heard the bad news.

parrot [par′ət] *n.* A brightly colored bird with a hooked bill, sometimes able to speak. ■

patchwork [pach′wûrk′] *adj.* Patterns of cloth in different colors or shapes sewed together in a design: The *patchwork* quilt has been in my family for many years.

perch [pûrch] **1** *n.* A place to sit: The bird was happy on its *perch* in the tree. **2** *v.* To sit: The bird will *perch* in the tree all night. **perched**

performance [pər·fôr′məns] *n.* An act done for an audience: The actors were ready for their first *performance.*

phonograph [fō′nə·graf] *n.* A machine that plays records: The school bought six new *phonographs* for our classrooms. *pl.* **phonographs** ■

photograph [fō′tə·graf] **1** *n.* A picture taken with a camera. *pl.* **photographs 2** *v.* To take pictures with a camera: She went to the zoo to *photograph* the animals. **photographed**

piano [pē·an′ō] *n.* A large musical instrument played by hitting keys with the fingers: He played the *piano* while she sang.

plow [plou] *v.* To break up and turn over the earth for planting: The farmer will *plow* his fields. ■

population [pop′yə·lā′shən] *n.* The number of people living in a place: The *population* of our town grows every year.

pottery [pot′ər·ē] *n.* Things, such as pots, made of clay and hardened by heat: Many people wanted to buy the beautiful *pottery.* ■

president [prez′ə·dent] *n.* The person who acts as head of a club or group: The *president* asked the people to take their seats.

proof [pro͞of] *n.* Something that shows that what was said is true: The detective had *proof* that the man had not been in the store.

protect [prə·tekt′] *v.* To keep or make safe: The tent will *protect* us from the rain. **protects**

protection [prə·tek′shən] *n.* A person or thing that protects: The cave was our *protection* from the storm.

prove [pro͞ov] *v.* To show something is true: He will *prove* that his answer is right.

prowler [proul′er] *n.* A person who watched for fires in the streets long ago. *pl.* **prowlers**

a	add	o	odd	oi	oil
ā	ace	ō	open	ou	pout
â	care	ô	order	ng	ring
ä	palm	o͝o	took	th	thin
e	end	o͞o	pool	th	this
ē	equal	u	up	zh	vision
i	it	û	burn		
ī	ice	yo͞o	fuse		

ə = { a in *above*, o in *melon*, e in *sicken*, u in *circus* }   i in *possible*

Q

quiet [kwī′ət] *n.* The state of having or making little noise: There was nothing but *quietness* in the house that night. **quietness**

R

radio [rā′dē·ō] *n.* A machine that sends sounds through the air from one place to another: Have you heard that new song on the *radio*? *pl.* **radios** ■

rate [rāt] *n.* The time in which something is done: At this *rate*, we will be home before dark.

realize [rē′əl·īz′] *v.* To understand: I *realize* that you will not be home for dinner. **realized**

reap [rēp] *v.* To bring in a crop: We *reaped* the crops before the rain started. **reaped**

rear-wheel [rir′-(h)wēl′] *adj.* Having to do with the back wheel: The *rear-wheel* tire was flat.

recognize [rek′əg·nīz] *v.* To see someone or something that is known: I will *recognize* the right road when we get there.

record [ri·kôrd′] **1** *v.* To put down for later use: Let's *record* that song so we can play it again. **recorded 2** *n.* **recorder** A machine used to play back things that have been recorded: We took a tape *recorder* with us on our trip. *pl.* **recorders**

reflector [ri·flekt′tər] *n.* Something that catches and shines back light that hits it: We could see the boat when our light shined on its *reflector.* ■

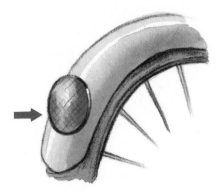

rehearsal [ri·hûr′səl] *n.* A practice performance: There was a special *rehearsal* before the play began.

rehearse [ri·hûrs′] *v.* To practice: The actors came to *rehearse* for the play. **rehearsed**

research [ri′sûrch] *n.* Careful study: It took many days of *research* to find out what really happened.

rhinoceros [rī·nos′ər·əs] *n.* A large animal with a thick skin and one or two horns: The children ran to the pen to look at the *rhinoceros.*

ringmaster [ring′mas′tər] *n.* The person in charge of the acts at a circus: The *ringmaster* told the audience about the dancing bears. ■

rush [rush] *v.* To hurry: We were *rushing* to get to the train on time. **rushing**

S

safety [sāf′tē] *adj.* Free from danger or harm: The driver wore a *safety* belt.

scary [skâr′ē] *adj.* Frightening: The children told each other *scary* stories.

scenery [sē′nər·ē] *n.* Paintings used to make a stage look like some other place: The *scenery* in the play made the stage look like a haunted house.

scream [skrēm] *v.* To give a long high cry, as in surprise: Try not to *scream* when the lights go out! **screamed**

second [sek′ənd] *n.* A small period of time: I will be ready in ten *seconds. pl.* **seconds**

settle [set′(ə)l] *v.* To become comfortable: She wanted to *settle* in the big chair and watch the show.

a	add	o	odd	oi	oil
ā	ace	ō	open	ou	pout
â	care	ô	order	ng	ring
ä	palm	o͝o	took	th	thin
e	end	o͞o	pool	t͟h	this
ē	equal	u	up	zh	vision
i	it	û	burn		
ī	ice	yo͞o	fuse		

ə = { a in *above*   e in *sicken*   i in *possible*
      o in *melon*   u in *circus* }

shaky [shāk′ ē] *adj.* Weak, unsteady: Her legs felt *shaky* as she walked across the wooden bridge.

shelter [shel′tər] *n.* Something that covers or protects: The deer looked for *shelter* in the forest.

slippery [slip′ər·ē] *adj.* Hard to hold or stand on: The road was *slippery* after the ice storm.

slope [slōp] *n.* Land that is not flat: The car started to roll down the *slope*.

sniffle [snif′əl] *v.* To breathe loudly through the nose: I heard my little brother *sniffle* because of his cold. **sniffled**

soccer [sok′ər] *n.* A game in which a ball is moved toward a goal by being kicked or hit with the body or head: The *soccer* game was very exciting.

spark [spärk] *n.* A small bit of fire: *Sparks* from the fire blew into the yard. *pl.* **sparks**

spill [spil] *n.* A fall: The racer took a *spill* on the turn.

spine [spīn] *n.* A hard, sharp part of a plant: Those cactus *spines* are sharp! *pl.* **spines**

sportsmanship [spôrts′mən·ship′] *n.* Fair play in games: The players showed good *sportsmanship*.

sprocket [sprok′it] *n.* One of a number of teeth on a wheel: The *sprocket* broke off when he rode the bike up the hill.

squawk [skwôk] *v.* To give a loud cry: The bird *squawked* when it was hungry. **squawked, squawking**

squeal [skwēl] *v.* To give a high cry: The pig *squealed* for its supper. **squealed**

squint [skwint] *v.* To look with eyes partly closed: She *squinted* when she first came out into the sun. **squinted**

stage [stāj] *n.* The raised place in a theater where a performance is given: The actors walked out onto the *stage*. ■

stamp [stamp] *v.* To hit hard with the feet: I *stamped* the floor to get the snow off my feet. **stamped**

steady [sted′ē] *adj.* Strongly set in place: He held the boat *steady* while we got in.

stretch [strech] *v.* To pull out or grow in size: He had to *stretch* his legs after sitting for so long.

stroke [strōk] *n.* The breaking of a blood vessel in the brain: He was in bed a long time after his *stroke*.

studio [st(y)oo′dē·ō] *n.* A place to work or teach, as for an artist: She painted many pictures in her *studio*. *pl.* **studios** ■

substitute [sub′stə·t(y)oot′] *n.* A person or thing that takes the place of someone or something else: Bob needed a *substitute* when he was hurt in the game.

suggest [sə(g)·jest′] *v.* To give an idea: I *suggest* we leave now. **suggests**

sunflower [sun′flou′ər] *n.* A tall plant with large flowers: The *sunflower* is the largest plant in our yard. *pl.* **sunflowers**

sunrise [sun′rīz′] *n.* The time when the sun comes up.

sunset [sun′set′] *n.* The time when the sun goes down.

survive [sər·vīv′] *v.* To live through: The plants will *survive* the storm.

swirl [swûrl] *v.* To move with a twisting motion: The wind made the leaves *swirl* up into the air. **swirling**

T

tailor [tā′lər] *n.* A person who makes or fixes clothes: The *tailor* made a new coat for me.

a	add	o	odd	oi	oil
ā	ace	ō	open	ou	pout
â	care	ô	order	ng	ring
ä	palm	ŏŏ	took	th	thin
e	end	ōō	pool	th	this
ē	equal	u	up	zh	vision
i	it	û	burn		
ī	ice	yōō	fuse		

ə = { a in *above*   e in *sicken*   i in *possible*
       o in *melon*   u in *circus* }

tangle [tang′gəl] *v.* To twist together: I watched the cat *tangle* the ball of yarn. **tangled**

thimble [thim′bəl] *n.* A metal or plastic cap worn to protect the finger in sewing: I needed a new *thimble*. ■

thousand [thou′zənd] *adj.* Ten hundreds, written as *1,000*: *Thousands* of people watched the ball game. *pl.* **thousands**

thread [thred] **1** *n.* Thin silk or cotton used for sewing: He used red *thread* to sew his shirt. **2** *v.* To put through a needle: It is not always easy to *thread* this needle. ■

thrill [thril] **1** *n.* A feeling of excitement: It was a big *thrill* to win the race. **2** *v.* To excite: Winning the prize will *thrill* me! **thrilled**

throat [thrōt] *n.* The front part of the neck: She had a sore *throat* this week.

throw [thrō] *v.* To make fly through the air: The ball was *thrown* high into the air. **thrown**

track [trak] *n.* A set path for racing: He ran ten laps around the *track*.

trade [trād] *v.* To give one thing for another: He will *trade* his van for the pickup truck.

treasure [trezh′ər] *n.* Things worth money, stored and kept carefully: The king's *treasure* room was guarded carefully. *pl.* **treasures**

twig [twig] *n.* A small branch of a tree: We looked for a long *twig* to draw a picture in the sand. *pl.* **twigs** ■

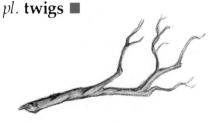

type [tīp] *v.* To hit keys on a machine that prints letters on paper: I have to *type* a letter before I go home. **types**

U

unanswered [un·an′sərd] *adj.* Not replied to: I have a pile of *unanswered* letters on my desk that I will read today.

unload [un·lōd′] *v.* To empty things from: The movers have *unloaded* the van. **unloaded**

unroll [un·rōl′] *v.* To open out: We *unrolled* the new rugs. **unrolled**

unusual [un·yoo′zhoo·əl] *adv.* Not common: The clown had a very *unusual* coat.

usual [yoo′zhoo·əl] *adj.* In the common or everyday way: We *usually* leave a light on at night. *adv.* **usually**

V

visitor [viz′ə·tər] *n.* A person that goes or comes to see someone or something: Last night we had *visitors*. *pl.* **visitors**

volume [vol′yəm] *n.* A book in a set: The school has one *volume* of his poems.

W

wink [wingk] *v.* To open and close the eyes: Michael *winked* at Betsy. **winked**

wooly [wŏŏl′ē] *adj.* Like the soft hair of a sheep: The *wooly* sweater kept me warm.

Z

zookeeper [zoo′kē′pər] *n.* A person who takes care of a zoo: The *zookeeper* knows a lot about many kinds of animals. ■

a	add	o	odd	oi	oil
ā	ace	ō	open	ou	pout
â	care	ô	order	ng	ring
ä	palm	ŏŏ	took	th	thin
e	end	oo	pool	th	this
ē	equal	u	up	zh	vision
i	it	û	burn		
ī	ice	yoo	fuse		

ə = { a in *above*   e in *sicken*   i in *possible*
      o in *melon*   u in *circus* }

323

Word List

The following words are introduced in this book. Each is listed beside the number of the page on which it first appears.

**Merle the
High-Flying Squirrel**
(4–13)

4   Merle
    traffic
    frightened
5   quietness
6   high-wire
7   realized
8   tangled
    untangle
    fierce
    caught
    tumble
9   tightened
    fast-moving
    whisper
10 whirlwind
    powerful
    crosswind
    sunset
11 redwood

Kites in Flight
(14–21)

14 thousand
16 plastic
    nylon
    materials

17 hundreds
18 flexi-kite
    novelty
19 flown
    Wright brothers
    Alexander
       Graham Bell

Newspapers
(24–25)

24 headline
    unnecessary
    attention
25 dateline
    byline
    research
    reporter

**The Bicycle
Balloon Chase**
(26–33)

26 bicycle
    Gina
27 Saturday
    pedaled
    Maple
    pedals
28 parrot
    aeronaut

    gondola
    unloaded
    bundle
    unrolled
30 dairy
    squawked
    Gypsy

Diagrams
(34–37)

34 diagrams
    explain
35 connected
    envelope
    inset
36 textbook
    application
    science
    easier
37 handlebars
    safety
    reflector
    attached
    sprocket

Bicycle Rider
(38–47)

38 Marshall Taylor
    Indianapolis

325

Key: (l) – Left; (r) – Right; (c) – Center; (t) – Top; (b) – Bottom

Photographs

Illustrators

7
C 8
D 9
E 0
F 1
G 2
H 3
I 4
J 5